*If the trumpet give an uncertain sound, who shall
prepare himself to the battle?*
—I Corinthians 14:8 (King James Version)

the series on school reform

Patricia A. Wasley
University of Washington

Ann Lieberman
Carnegie Foundation for the
Advancement of Teaching

Joseph P. McDonald
New York University

SERIES EDITORS

(Continued)

MOBILIZING CITIZENS
for
BETTER SCHOOLS

Robert F. Sexton

Foreword by Richard W. Riley

Teachers College, Columbia University
New York and London

Published by Teachers College Press, 1234 Amsterdam Avenue, New York, NY 10027

Library of Congress Cataloging-in-Publication Data

Sexton, Robert F.
   Mobilizing citizens for better schools / Robert F. Sexton ; foreword by
Richard W. Riley.
     p. cm. — (The series on school reform)
   Includes bibliographical references and index.
   ISBN 0-8077-4442-5 (cloth) — ISBN 0-8077-4441-7 (pbk.)
    1. School improvement programs—Kentucky. 2. Education and
state—Kentucky. 3. Educational change—Kentucky. 4. Prichard Committee
for Academic Excellence. I. Title. II. Series.
   LB2822.83.K4S49 2004
   379.796—dc22   2003064596

ISBN:0-8077-4441-7 (paper)
ISBN:0-8077-4442-5 (cloth)

Printed on acid-free paper
Manufactured in the United States of America

11 10 09 08 07 06 05 04   8 7 6 5 4 3 2 1

Contents

Foreword

The future of our great country depends on how effective we are in bringing about constant improvement in our schools. Under our system of government, this is the responsibility of each of the 50 states. The federal and local governments have important roles, but the actual responsibility rests with the states.

The state of Kentucky has dealt with this challenge in a very interesting, unique, and dramatic way, and the Prichard Committee for Academic Excellence has played a major role in Kentucky's education story. We are so fortunate that Bob Sexton, who helped establish the Committee more than 20 years ago and has been a key leader through its many critical stages, now shares his clear account with us.

Public engagement is absolutely essential to make school reform successful. This book is a study of public engagement told in a helpful way by someone who has been on the front line for two decades.

To have effective public involvement, a state must lay a firm foundation, get focused, and stay engaged over time. Bob Sexton catalogues the Kentucky experience, providing suggestions for success and then illustrating them with real examples. He backs up his experiences with wise and helpful observations from respected educators and education researchers.

I have known about the Prichard Committee since I was Governor of South Carolina during the 1980s and spearheading education reform there. In 1989, the Supreme Court of Kentucky declared that state's entire system of common schools to be unconstitutional. The following year Kentucky enacted one of the most sweeping and comprehensive school reforms in the nation. That system remains in place today and, on indicators such as the National Assessment of Educational Progress, Kentucky's student achievement has improved steadily since 1990.

I continued to follow the efforts of the Prichard Committee while I was U.S. Secretary of Education and, when visiting Louisville in 1997, met with Committee members to discuss education reform.

From my experience as Secretary and as Governor, I am convinced that strong, sustainable education improvement requires the engagement and mobilization of parents, business people and the public at large—they must demand, own, and protect reform. However, no matter how personally concerned and interested the people are, they need information and leadership to succeed. The Prichard Committee—itself a group of volunteer citizens—has provided this leadership in Kentucky. It is hard to imagine how education reform as dramatic as Kentucky's could have been launched, much less sustained over time, without the Committee's leadership.

Bob Sexton has written a book for activists who want to mobilize parental, business, and other public support for education. This is not an academic tome. It is filled with practical advice supported by his personal reflections and stories. It tells us much about the most active period of education change in American history.

Richard W. Riley
Former U.S. Secretary of Education
Former Governor of South Carolina

Acknowledgments

I owe deep thanks to my friends, colleagues and family for their attention and assistance over the years. They have helped with their ideas, with moral and financial support, and with the preparation of this book manuscript.

This book would have been no more than a notion without the support of the late Mary Bingham and the Bingham Foundation of Louisville, which allowed me to spend a sabbatical as a visiting scholar in the Graduate School of Education at Harvard University. My hosts and colleagues there—Richard Elmore, Bob Schwartz, Jay Braatz, and many others—gave me the encouragement and environment I needed to take writing this story seriously. I am grateful to them.

Many people have helped with observations, reactions, or research that have shaped my thinking. Several of these are cited in the references, but I owe a few special acknowledgment: Jacob Adams, Norm Fruchter, Molly Hunter, Tom James, Steve Kay, Frank Newman, Janice Petrovich, Wendy Puriefoy, Mike Rebell, Rona Roberts, and Susan Traiman. Joe McDonald deserves special thanks. He has encouraged this project from the start and has generously offered his advice on more than one draft of the manuscript.

The superb editorial and organizational skills of Diana Taylor, along with her friendship, have been instrumental in the completion of the book. I am also grateful to Holly Holland who assisted in important ways in the early stages. The preparation of the final manuscript was carried out by members of the skilled Prichard Committee staff; Michelle Whitaker and Pam Shepherd deserve my special thanks for their talents and patience, and I am also grateful to Melody Slusher, Janet Jones, and Susan Curtiss. Other Prichard Committee staff members have been immensely supportive and I appreciate them all deeply.

My friends and allies, the citizen volunteers on the Prichard Committee, have my personal thanks and admiration for their years of dedicated commitment. They have been and still are the ultimate builders of social capital. Without them there would be no story to tell. One Committee member, the first among many special people, my wife Pamela Sexton, has been there for 23 years. The Committee and its work has been our common cause more than most people can ever know.

Introduction

I didn't know I could do that.
—Parent, Commonwealth Institute for Parent Leadership

This is the story of a group of parents and citizens who decided to improve the schools in their state. Those volunteers and I commenced about 20 years ago and are still at it. Many people have asked what we have learned, and I decided that telling our story could be useful.

WHAT IS THE PRICHARD COMMITTEE?

The Prichard Committee for Academic Excellence was established as an independent, private corporation in 1983. Before that, from 1980 until 1983, it was a commission of citizens appointed by the Kentucky Council on Higher Education and called the Committee on Higher Education in Kentucky's Future. The 30 citizen members of that group, chaired by attorney Edward F. Prichard, decided after issuing their report on higher education to recreate themselves as an independent, nonprofit, nonpartisan, citizens' organization. They did so because they were frustrated with elected officials' indifference to education and because they felt that Kentucky's historic educational deficits would not solve themselves. They were sick of complacency. They wanted to create a compelling vision of a future with excellent schools.

These days when people discuss public engagement they often focus on what schools or school districts need to do. Their view is that school administrators need to reach out to the public, inform them, and urge consensus around their agendas. The report of a recent Wingspread conference is a good example of this: "Schools should make continuous efforts and provide endless opportunities to get parents involved—always invite" (Duggan & Holmes, 2000, p. 15).

But that wasn't the case in the early days of the independent Prichard Committee. No one in education "invited" the volunteer Prichard Committee members to do anything. They invited themselves. Their approach was outside-in not inside-out as they set out to make education quality the central public concern for other Kentuckians. We saw serious problems, and we decided to make noise about them.

The committee's staff between 1983 and 1990 consisted of a director and a secretary. Before 1990, financial support came entirely from Kentucky businesses and individuals; after 1990, about 80 percent came from national foundations. Funding, not surprisingly, has been a constant struggle. As of this writing, the committee consists of about 100 volunteer members with a staff of 20 and an extended family of volunteers and friends numbering several thousand.

So the Prichard Committee is a citizen voice. It has a staff, offices, publications, and the like. But it is, first and foremost, a group of citizens—a committee. It cannot, of course, *be* all citizens or *speak for* all citizens. However, it can speak for the citizens who voluntarily give it their time, endorsement, encouragement, or financial support. Its extended family is open to all who agree with its stated purpose, namely, the improvement of education for Kentuckians of all ages.

Someone once said that the Prichard Committee translates ideas to the public. Partly true, but not fully accurate either. As an assembly of volunteer citizens, the committee is, in small part, the public itself. The group operates at both the grassroots and policy levels at the same time. Whenever possible, the citizens on the committee or other volunteers do the work themselves.

As activists, the members of the Prichard Committee concluded that the state's seemingly intractable problems in education could not be solved solely through governmental actions. They strategized that the state also needed a reinvestment in civic capital; their fellow citizens needed to speak up. They were willing to consider new questions and alternatives, to educate themselves about the issues, to practice the skills of citizenship, and to teach those skills to others and encourage them to use them. They decided to take personal responsibility for changing the state's direction in education instead of viewing it as somebody else's job. And they decided to stick with the job over time.

CONDITIONS THAT SHAPED OUR WORK

Several years ago a friend from another state brought a group of business and foundation leaders to visit the Prichard Committee to find out what we had done. They wanted to create a similar organization in their state. They met for hours with our staff and volunteers. They reviewed materials. After 2 days they left, appearing sated and energized. Months later I asked my friend how his group was doing. Was it now a mobilized group of school reform advocates? Had their visit been helpful? "It was helpful," he said, "but we've shut down. After talking to you, we decided it was too hard."

What I describe here is not easy to do.

Political organizing is unique to place—to local culture, history, and demographics. Although the experiences I write about here have occurred in one state, the lessons taught by those experiences have application elsewhere. In this chapter I'll give a road map of the story ahead, including a few twists in the path. However, several conditions shape this story and need some explanation in advance.

Kentucky's School Reform

First, the Prichard Committee's story becomes, after 1990, intertwined with the story of the Kentucky Education Reform Act, passed by the legislature that year and still being implemented today. Although this book is not the story of that reform, there are many lessons to be learned from its implementation and from the Prichard Committee's role in it—lessons germane to organizing in a systemic, standards-based reform environment. But readers who want a full analysis of Kentucky's school reform will need to look elsewhere; there are suggestions for further reading at the conclusion of the book.

Many people believe the Prichard Committee was created after the Kentucky Education Reform Act was passed to monitor or promote its implementation. Not so; the committee predated the reform by 10 years. The Prichard Committee's self-chosen mission since the early 1980s has been to promote vastly improved education for all Kentuckians. With that as our goal, we were pragmatists when it came to specific reforms. Our main questions about any specific reform proposal since the mid-1980s have been: "Will it improve Kentucky schools? Will it improve student achievement?" In our second major report (Prichard Committee, 1987) we argued for a comprehensive, sweeping approach and for vastly increased funding for schools. Our view of a comprehensive approach emphasized preschool, dealing with child poverty and other barriers to learning, improved teacher preparation and professional development, and much more. The "much more" would have looked, to an outside observer, like what was then called *systemic reform* and articulated in the 1980s by reform theorists like Marc Tucker, Mike Smith, and Jennifer O'Day.

When Kentucky's reform was passed in 1990, it was seen as a dramatic example of systemic and comprehensive reform. Reforms like Kentucky's have since been labeled *standards-based*, and that is a fair description of the reform context in which the Prichard Committee operates. Even though we did not create the Prichard Committee as an advocate for any particular brand of reform, the direction Kentucky has taken (standards, assessment, accountability, local decision making, professional development, increased funding, and so forth) has positioned us within that reform approach.

Even though our organization is known because of its connection to Kentucky's school reform initiative, what we have learned can apply to any school reform environment. We created the independent Prichard Committee in 1983, long before Kentucky's reform was enacted, to pursue the mission of vastly improving education for all Kentuckians. Important lessons grew from those years and, as it turns out, we now know that we were laying the groundwork for what happened in 1990.

The issues around testing and accountability have changed so much since 1990 that they lead to confusion about state reforms, so an explanation is needed before we begin. Today in many states, but not in Kentucky or about 20 other states, state tests and accountability applies to students, determining whether they progress from grade to grade or graduate. Predictably, these consequences for students have opened up new kinds of controversies about testing around the country. Those controversies are not a factor in our story.

I also need to set the context about changing political labels and avoid confusion for the reader. Alan Wolfe calls the current situation the "topsy-turvy world of school reform," where the political climate has been muddied and the political language people use turned on its head. In the early 1990's reformers were blasted as "leftists" by the "right," says Wolfe, and indeed we were, but that has changed:

> To the degree that education remains a hotly contested political issue, we will increasingly see odd political alliances: hippies and conservative Christians in favor of home-schooling, African-Americans and white Catholics in favor of vouchers, old-fashioned leftists and political conservatives in favor of standards, multi-culturists and advertisers in favor of relevance. (2000, p. 40)

The "Public Engagement" Conversation Around the Country

The second condition that affects this book is the increasing national conversation about the critical role an engaged public must play if

American public schools are to educate all students well. In my view, this conversation reflects two different perspectives. One is alarm, and it is heard in the voices of writers such as David Mathews (1996), who contend that the public writ large has lost both its interest and its commitment to public schools. They worry about the future since a public that is AWOL undermines a basic American institution and will forecast, if not turned around, further public school deterioration. The other perspective is more hopeful. It comes from people who are busy tapping the well of citizens who do care a lot about their public schools and who are, or can be, actively engaged. These advocates labor with the complexities and difficulties of seriously changing schools and, to do so, are figuring out how the public can help with the challenge. This perspective is found in the rhetoric and programs of organizations like the Public Education Network, the Education Trust, and the Annenberg Institute; in foundations like BellSouth, Ford, and Casey; and in the writings of people like Clarence Stone, Tony Wagner, Dick Elmore, and others.

My interest and experience put us with this latter, more hopeful, group. Finding an effective way to build civic capacity and engage the public is the subject of this book. By testing our experience against research and theory, and by explaining what we have done and how we have done it, I hope others might be more successful in mobilizing the public as a force for school improvement.

Distrust of Government and Politics

The nation's current policy-making climate is the third condition that affects this story. The Prichard Committee's lessons unfold in the context of Americans' changing attitudes toward government and involvement in politics and civic life. Researchers tell us that across the nation there has been an erosion of consensus, a fragmentation of opinion, and a distrust of public institutions that have emerged as powerful negative forces. "We have found a marked decline in trust (in government) over the past three decades" concludes Gary Orren in *Why People Don't Trust Government*, with a majority of Americans believing that "government action is doomed to failure" (1997, p. 85). Meanwhile, people's lists of what they want government to do and pay for keep growing.

Likewise, the civic and political climate turned sour—one of the "nastiest decades in American political history," one scholar called the 1990s (Mayer, 2002, p. 6). Political discourse has become bitterly polarized and politicians less inclined toward moderation. Terms like *civic disengagement, public cynicism, argument culture,* and *culture of disrespect* described the age. Media coverage of issues changed dramatically as the public attention span shrunk and sound-bite journalism prevailed; even sound bites themselves shrunk—from 48 seconds per political ad in 1968 to 7 seconds per ad today (Page, 1996).

This isn't good news for anyone mobilizing citizens to initiate or support reform in public schools—by definition, a government function. If most people think that government services cannot be improved or changed, and that government is at best ineffective and at worst an evil empire, what do you do if your job is to improve it? If, as Richard Neustadt writes, high levels of mistrust "can help render governance hard, frustrating, and sluggish, something akin to traversing a field covered in molasses" (1997, p. 181), how does a group like the Prichard Committee go about doing its job?

These three conditions—school reform, public engagement in education reform, and distrust of government—are a constant presence and have shaped what we have done. But they are not the main event. Instead, this book tells a story that is germane today because of the current status of school reform across the nation—particularly large-scale and long-term reforms like so-called standards-based reform—and the strong upswing of interest in public engagement as a factor in that reform movement.

WHY DOES THE PUBLIC MATTER?

The Prichard Committee predates the nation's current fixation on so-called systemic reform or standards-based reform. In the 20 years that have followed our beginning, the dialogue has changed from a focus on reforms like merit pay and tougher course requirements to assessment and accountability, school-based decision making, incentives, and capacity building. Reform based on high standards and accountability for student learning now is in full flood. With this wave also has come a wave of activist and scholarly interest in the public's role, referred to as *public engagement, civic capacity,* or *public will.*

Sometimes I hear discussions of public engagement that sound something like this: "The transformation of schools so all children learn at high levels is a difficult and complex business. These difficulties are grossly underestimated by most people. Voters, parents, and taxpayers will make decisions whether they are informed or not, so it's better that they be informed of what the schools are planning to do."

Sometimes I even hear tones of surprise, as if it's a revelation that the public needs to be involved for reforms to be successful. It has always struck me as odd that anyone would be surprised. Why would they ever have thought, I wonder, that school reform could happen without people outside schools being involved?

But recently we see scholars taking civic capacity more seriously. There is evidence of this in the writing of Anne Henderson, Richard Elmore, Paul Hill, Michael Fullan, Susan Fuhrman, David Evans, Linda Darling-Hammond, Clarence Stone, and other academics. Researchers who have varied perspectives about the most effective reform strategies seem to agree on the importance of an engaged and supportive public if reforms are to be successful. "Every community embarking on a school reform strategy needs a long-lasting civic reform oversight group," wrote Paul Hill (2001, p. 11).

One of the most obvious, and thoroughly researched, connections involves parents. In *A New Generation of Evidence: The Family is Critical to Student Achievement*, Anne Henderson and Nancy Berla wrote: "The evidence is beyond dispute. When schools work together with families to support learning, children tend to succeed not just in school, but throughout life. . . . When parents are involved in their children's education at home, the children do better in school. When parents are involved in school, they go farther in school, and schools they go to are better" (1994, p. 1).

The public we are concerned with, however, goes beyond parents. So do the findings of other scholars. Jay Braatz and Robert Putnam posit that "schools can't do it alone. . . . The evidence in this paper, as well as the long tradition of close connections between schools and communities, lends credence to the view that revitalizing American civic engagement may be a prerequisite for revitalizing American education" (1998, p. 37).

But the truism that schools can't do it alone leaves unanswered a more complicated question. Do close public connections in themselves guarantee schools that are rigorous, that try to teach every child well, and that have high student achievement? Of course not. So it is important to consider the links between reform and public engagement in their more complex form.

The essays by University of Maryland political scientist Clarence Stone, in his collection *Changing Urban Education*, are essential reading. Stone's research leads him to claim that "the connections between level of civic capacity and degree of effort at education improvement seems quite solid" (1998, p. 261). Stone's chosen term, *civic capacity*, means to him "mobilization of varied stakeholders in support of a community-wide cause" (p. 261). Stone sees civic capacity as having two defining elements: contributing in some way to the cause (participation or involvement) and "understanding," or seeing that an issue is a community problem that calls for collective action. As an ideal, he argues that "civic capacity entails not simply bringing a coalition together around the issue of educational improvement but beyond that engaging the members in activities and promoting discourse" (p. 258).

Why is civic capacity so important? Because introducing reform is a political act and the status quo, with strong defenders, has the advantage. Reform's beneficiaries are an "undependable body of supporters" and reform is only a distant possibility. "Moreover," writes Stone in a key observation, "in today's climate, reforms run up against a high degree of skepticism about whether planned change can actually work. Indifference and disbelief are formidable barriers, and small but determined opposition can feed both" (1998, p. 7).

In sum, writes Stone—consistent with our own experience—the political challenge is to build a *"new set of political arrangements commensurate with the policy being advocated"* where academic performance is the *"focal concern"* (1998, p. 9, italics in original).

The writings of Harvard's Richard Elmore, one of the most insightful scholars analyzing the complex reforms that are sweeping the nation, are particularly useful in showing where the public fits into the reform equation. Elmore is effective in drawing forth the "central dilemmas of large-scale reforms," as he calls them. In an essay for the Business Roundtable, he helps us realize that stakes are higher today than they were 50 years ago because we expect much more of schools. The challenge is massive and new to American education. "We can produce many examples of how educational practice could look different, but we can produce few, if any, examples of large numbers of teachers engaging in these practices in large-scale institutions designed to deliver education to most children" (1996, p. 308).

For Elmore, the problem grows from the complexities of changing schools for the better and from the inadequacies of past reforms. What usually happened when reforms were implemented in the past? Schools "add new programs, they develop highly visible initiatives that respond to prevailing opinions in the community, they open new units in the organization to accommodate new clients. . . . But the core patterns of schooling remain relatively stable in the face of often massive changes in the structure around them" (1996, p. 313). In short, they rename what they were doing before and just keep on going.

The reform climate is the key to success, says Elmore. If, as in

Kentucky, the goal is to reach all classrooms and improve performance for all children, the reform climate must be more powerful and sustained longer than ever before. Essential to this climate and to improving all schools, not just a few schools, are powerful connections between "big ideas and the fine grain of practice in the core of schooling" (1996, p. 317). But the capacity to make those connections waxes and wanes depending on who's in charge. Little is in place to keep attention focused over time. Cycles of trial and error result. Even the most committed teachers who try to do new and more effective work may not know what to do. The magnitude of the task requires that we "not expect to see immediate large-scale adoption of promising new practices . . . because the problems of scale are deeply rooted in the incentives and cultural norms of the institutions and cannot be fixed with single policy shifts or exhortations from people with money" (p. 327).

For school reform advocates, Elmore's most helpful insight leads to something like a golden rule: Stay focused over time because no one else will. The core political problem, says Elmore, is that day-to-day political strategies are usually built on "exhortation" not on sustaining a reform climate.

Elmore emphasizes that the political clock runs faster than the school-change clock. Immediate results are what elected officials want to take home to their constituents, but the complexities of school improvement require time to implement and show results. Indeed, the process never ends as teachers, administrators, parents, and community members sort out what works and what doesn't. For politicians 2 or maybe 4 years is the limit, and then they want to move on; the school-change clock runs at a much slower pace.

So one thing that is needed is time. But who can buy it? In my view it is only an organization that can stand back from election cycles and take a long view.

About 5 years into implementing the 1990 Kentucky reform, a friend said, "What the Prichard Committee does is buy time for the system to ingest the reforms." What he meant by "ingesting" is what Elmore meant by "breaking cycles of trial and error." This essential challenge, which may require decades (mega-lifetimes in political terms), is not something government agencies or elected officials can provide. It's not their job; they're not equipped to do it. A focus on change, plus longevity and continuity over time, must come from some entity with capacities that are not present in government or elected bodies.

We've thought a lot about time. It shapes all our campaign strategies. One of our volunteer members observed, "I think the most important judgment you made was seeing the passage of the Kentucky Education Reform Act not as the light at the end of the tunnel, but as the beginning of the light at the end of the tunnel." He was talking about a core challenge for any advocacy group: giving itself enough staying power—time—and convincing the public that change cannot come quickly.

Another scholar who has studied the public's role in reform is Susan Fuhrman, Director of the Consortium for Policy Research in Education. She has found that engagement over time is required because our political machinery isn't adequate for long-term, coherent policy implementation. Most reforms need to be implemented over considerable time and guided by "a series of key policies that should be aligned with outcome expectations." Politics, though, doesn't work that way. "Consensual decision making and policy coordination have seemed beyond the capacity of our political system. In fact, it is arguable that our political system functions so to deliberately thwart decisiveness and coordination" (1994, p. 2).

Fuhrman sees four specific political conditions as barriers to reform: fragmented organization, election cycles, policy overload, and specialization. She finds that independent organizations, external to government and with staying power, have helped to overcome these four barriers in the states she studied. For instance, by articulating a clear vision powerfully, independent organizations can cut across the lines of fragmented decision making (legislative, executive, local school district) and force a focus on common reform objectives. Such organizations can "bridge traditional divisions," such as those between unions and administrators, by bringing them together for dialogue. They can link diverse constituencies together in a credible public voice, not beholden to one single constituency. Such organizations can also smooth out the disruption of elections and election cycles by focusing attention on what's important, not what's immediate, and by setting priorities for candidates. They can also be the institutional memory bridging changes in administrations. Finally, credible independent organizations can keep public attention focused on reform. By reporting on problems and progress, and by focusing attention on existing policy and what needs changing, they can give elected officials a way of showing they care about education without veering off to totally new policies and programs. If these things are done, says Fuhrman, there "are fewer shifts in emphasis and less proliferation of projects," and reform's direction is more likely to be maintained over time (1994, p. 6).

Fuhrman's observations might apply to all independent organizations, not just public advocacy groups made up of citizen volunteers like the Prichard Committee. Many organizations can provide the coherence and continuity Fuhrman values. What is unique about citizens' groups, as opposed to staff-driven organizations, trade groups, or professional associations, emerges from the story in this book.

Those who study the change process suggest other ways of looking at the role of reform-minded citizens' organizations. One of these is Michael Fullan. "There can be little doubt that the mobilization of large numbers of caring adults is absolutely central to the chances of success," he writes (1993, p. 6). Political stability over time is a key for Fullan as it is for Fuhrman and Stone. The challenge of reform is

> to engage in continuously corrective analysis and action. Productive education change, at its core, is not the capacity to implement the latest policy, but rather the ability to survive the vicissitudes of planned and unplanned change while growing and developing. . . . Teachers cannot do this job alone. . . . We must ingrain in society the kind of capacity for educational change that inevitably generates its own checks and balances and lines of solutions in situations that will always be somewhat out of control, even if we do everything right. (Fullan, 1993, pp. 5–7)

Fullan, it seems to me, is saying that school personnel need both civic pressure *and* support. An independent organization can "reassure educators that their stress, anguish, and even bitterness is acknowledged and remind them that it is a natural part of the change process. People will not venture into uncertainty unless they or others appreciate that difficulties are a natural part of any change scenario" (p. 25).

Others voice similar views. Henry Healey and Joseph DeStefano in *Education Reform Support: A Framework for Scaling Up School Reform*, written for the Center for International Development, argue that reform must be "demand driven" and home grown. A "sense of ownership enhances the overall implementability of reform. Significant parent and public engagement is essential" (1997, p. 9).

Another perspective comes from teacher education advocate Linda Darling-Hammond, who acknowledges that public discourse is critical since "without engaging parents, communities, and educators in sustained discussion about the schools we want and the teaching we need, no research-based reform can succeed widely for very long" (1998, p. 5).

Scholars argue that, for standards-based reform, an engaged public is particularly critical. The Committee on Title I Testing and Assessment argues that for assessment to drive achievement gains,

> everyone in the system—students, parents, teachers, administrators, and policy makers at every level—needs high-quality information about the quality of instruction and student performance. At the same time, everyone needs to be responsible for fulfilling his or her role in improving results. The key is transparency: everyone should know what is expected, what they will be measured on, and what the results imply for what they should do next. (National Research Council, 1999, p. 3)

We agree. Improving student achievement is heavy lifting, and the public needs to help. Community accountability is just as important as school accountability for today's standards-based reforms to succeed. We spend lots of time showing the public—parents in particular—that they have a role. As we train parents in our Commonwealth Institute for Parent Leadership (see Chapter 7), we want them to understand and know how to use the assessment data their schools receive from the state department of education. We tell them that a core concept of standards-based reform is that achievement data must be useful, that data is sent to schools so something will happen and guide improved practice. "Your role," we say, "is to be sure that happens." Getting results for all children cannot be left to educators alone.

A GROWTH INDUSTRY: PUBLIC ENGAGEMENT

Learning about public engagement is a growth industry these days. The Harvard Graduate School of Education, for example, sponsors an institute each year on engaging the public in public schools. State groups like New York's Campaign for Fiscal Equity (CFE) have implemented public engagement strategies to support their legal strategies. Kentucky's combination of legal and political mobilization, described in detail by Michael Paris (2001) and Molly Hunter (1999), was taken to a new level of sophistication by Mike Rebell as he fashioned the New York campaign. No haphazard strategist, Rebell and his colleagues have carefully analyzed engagement strategies across the country (ACCESS, 2001).

Foundations such as the Ford Foundation have grant programs focused on constituency building. National organizations like the Business Roundtable spend great amounts of time and money on business-led reform organizations. The BellSouth Foundation sponsors a network of state-level advocacy organizations called the Columbia

Group. The Public Education Network, led by president Wendy Purie-foy, found through opinion research that "Americans are genuinely willing to get personally involved to make their schools better," so they have started a major engagement initiative (Puriefoy, 2000, p. 36).

This energy and interest, plus curiosity about Kentucky education reform, has led to increased interest in the Prichard Committee itself. New York advocates for fiscal equity, write Leibman and Sabel, "draw explicitly on the experience of the Prichard Committee in Kentucky" (2003, p. 109). Bruno Manno of the Annie E. Casey Foundation has said of Kentucky and the Prichard Committee: "You've created a new set of institutions that we now know are needed to sustain an education reform effort [of] the magnitude of what you're trying here" (2000, p. 3).

New York University political scientist Marilyn Gittell, in her book *Strategies for School Equity*, cites Kentucky as having implemented the "only statewide comprehensive reform resulting from a court decision on equity funding." The Prichard Committee's role in the reforms, she writes, is "a remarkable example of successful implementation of a court action that resulted at least in part from sustained coalition-building with organized parent and community activism and vital corporate support" (1998, p. 237). A case study from the Harvard Family Research Project calls the Committee "one of the best known and most successful public engagement initiatives in the country" (2000, p. 1).

Along with this attention, the Prichard Committee has also received plenty of credit, or blame, for what's happened in Kentucky schools. David Hornbeck, for instance, reflecting on the passage of Kentucky's reform in 1990, said, "It simply would not have happened if the Prichard Committee had not laid the groundwork so that people could even think that it was possible to do what the General Assembly did" (2000).

FINAL THOUGHTS

Surprises and curves in the road are all but guaranteed in complex social endeavors. This being so, I want to be cautious about sounding like everything we did was carefully planned in advance or that this book contains a blueprint to be followed. What we learned was more from trial and error, from seeing what works, than from any rational planning process.

Scholars who study large-scale policy problems where solutions are unclear have even coined a term for what I am describing: *the science of muddling through.* Yale political scientist James Scott captured this spirit well when he advised policy makers that the "step by step 'muddling through' approach would seem to be the only prudent course in . . . public policy implementation, where surprises are all but guaranteed" (1998, pp. 327–329).

There are indeed rules of thumb that bear on success. But the knowledge we've gained from muddling through is also difficult to explain in a way that is useful to others, a common worry for practitioners like me. The learning here comes from doing—by feel, intuition, false starts, and lessons learned over time. That's the spirit in which this book is written.

The first chair of the Prichard Committee, one of my partners in creating it, liked to inspire his colleagues with a verse from First Corinthians: "If the trumpet give an uncertain sound, who shall prepare himself to the battle?" This book is about how the Prichard Committee made a certain sound, how it prepared for battle, and what kind of battle it was.

I have tried to tell a story that will be useful to readers who have a wide range of experiences with school reform and with organizing public support for improved schools. This audience includes local activists, business leaders, and philanthropists or politicians who want to create movements of their own or those who are already deeply involved—the hundreds of reformers in dozens of movements already under way. That audience also includes scholars who study and write about the politics of education or the condition of civic life in America. For this latter group, it is my view that mobilizing and organizing strategies have more commonalities than differences across fields that range from health care to child welfare, to education. Thus this story also offers lessons for anyone involved in any citizen-engagement process, regardless of the cause.

This book is not a history of the Prichard Committee for Academic Excellence. I have pulled episodes and lessons from that experience, but I have left out details that would be included in a traditional history. Instead, it is a study of public engagement, told from the perspective of someone who has been involved in a successful effort for more than 2 decades.

There are lessons here, but the reader should not be looking for a cookbook in these pages. Instead, I find much to agree with in Richard Harwood's words, "Engaging the public realm is more about gaining perspective and understanding than about memorizing and implementing a step-by-step plan" (1996, p. 7).

It is important to note that this story is not about one person's effort. What has been and continues to be done through the Prichard Committee is the work of many people. It is fundamental in the public sphere that leaders help people think through problems they may or may not know they have and the solutions they will support. It is also fundamental, especially since volunteers' rewards are usually intangible and personal, that people get the credit they deserve.

A saying on a friend's office wall reads: "We have all drunk from wells we did not dig." That thought has driven my approach to working with the Prichard Committee. It also drives the approach of this book.

What will you find as you turn these pages? I begin with reflections about the timeliness of the Prichard Committee's lessons and where they fit with both school reform and concerns about civil society today. I summarize the operating principles that have driven our work and decisions, following that with a brief summary of the Prichard Committee's experience to provide context. Finally, I suggest lessons for success and illustrate them with examples from our experience.

My objective throughout has been to provide enough detail for those who ask "What should I do?" and for those who want to know more about the politics of reform. To make the lessons and story flow, I have omitted specific names, places, and circumstances, details that would not be useful to readers outside of Kentucky.

The committee's story naturally divides itself into three parts:

- The initial stage was getting organized and successfully launching our organization. This occurred between 1980 and 1983, when the Prichard Committee began as a state-appointed blue-ribbon commission focused on higher education.
- Next came the transition to an independent, private, nonprofit, non-partisan group of citizens. In that period, 1983–1990, our hope was to rouse our fellow parents and citizens, making school improvement a premier political concern.
- The third stage began with the Kentucky Education Reform Act in 1990. With reform laws in place, implementation became the focus. All the rules changed. The citizens' job now was not demanding reform, but buying time for new policies to take root and be accepted by educators, to help policies move from the legislature into the classroom.

Each period contains lessons about engaging citizens. The transition to the third stage proved the most challenging and may be the most useful to today's reader. Before 1990, the committee and other citizens raised questions and made noise about poor quality education and made recommendations based on public deliberation. Following passage of the reform legislation, the committee's volunteer members decided to keep going but to redesign their agenda. They saw their new job as keeping the public involved and vigilant, promoting the thoughtful implementation of the reform, informing the public and the business community, monitoring the reform's progress, and making recommendations for either additional reforms or for changes in the new law.

Not surprisingly, we learned that it was one thing to complain and demand, but it was another to encourage implementation of a complex and controversial array of detailed policies. It was, as our chairperson was fond of saying, "easier to throw stones than to catch them."

CHAPTER 1

Getting Started

We felt betrayed. Some people hadn't made good on their promises,
and we decided we had to fight back.
        —Dot Ridings, Prichard Committee Chair

The organization that is now known for its role in Kentucky's 1990 education reform actually began in 1980 with an interest in higher education. It all started when 30 people were appointed by the Kentucky Council on Higher Education (the state's coordinating body for public universities) to make recommendations about the future of Kentucky higher education. After an invigorating 18 months spent debating issues and writing a report that captured the attention of the media and the higher education community—a report a scholar called "unquestionably the best report written by any group in 3 decades"—these volunteers' spirits dropped to a low point when politicians declined to act. "We were mad as hell," said one of the original 30 members (Parrish, 1990, pp. 11, 16). The experience of that initial committee shaped what has been sustained for more than 20 years since.

This group was conceived and appointed in the traditional way. "Our public universities are fraught with problems, so let's appoint a blue ribbon committee to tell us what we need to do," was the rough reasoning. I was hired to organize this initiative.

When I was asked to join the council's staff as deputy director of policy and planning, I was an administrator at the University of Kentucky. The new job was an exciting fit with my interests. My academic degree was in modern U.S. history, and my research interest was Kentucky politics. At the university, my role was to help improve undergraduate education, to improve teaching quality, and to make learning more exciting and important inside a research institution.

My passion and talent was getting things started. In today's parlance I see now that I was essentially an entrepreneur, albeit a civic one.

Heading an initiative to reform all of higher education fit beautifully with my entrepreneurial and organizing bent. The job brought together my passion for improving higher education, for innovation and policy, with my self-defined role as a change agent. So in 1980 I left the university to plan and organize the new blue ribbon Committee on Higher Education in Kentucky's Future.

All the seeds of what later became the Prichard Committee for Academic Excellence were planted in the first 20 months (1980–1982) of that officially appointed and authorized group. The planning and strategies we used, the decisions we made, and the style we adopted defined the character of the fully independent body we created in 1983, the Prichard Committee.

SELECTING MEMBERS AND A CHAIR

Membership and leadership were the first critical decisions. We decided that a highly regarded noneducator should chair the group. That ultimately led us to Edward F. Prichard, Jr. A Harvard educated attorney and former Felix Frankfurter law clerk and New Dealer, Prichard had become a legendary public intellectual. He was a political insider and adviser to governors, a friend of presidents and publishers, like Katharine Graham of the *Washington Post*, who described the youthful Prichard as the "the most impressive man of our generation, the one who dazzled us most" (Campbell, 1998, p. 2). Above all, Prichard was an eloquent and outspoken advocate for high-quality higher education. He brought immense credibility, intellectual power, eloquence, and contacts to the process.

With Prichard in place we filled out the group's membership with 30 other volunteers, all private citizens. These included visible statewide leaders in business, former elected officials, and local or regional activists.

Vital to the group were people who would take the work seriously, folks who knew about advocacy. Local and regional activists were important for this reason. Many of these were women, and several had organizing experience with the League of Women Voters or other local groups. We expected these women to push the group, to be attentive to process, and to demand results. They also knew how to take the initiative and get things done. One example, out of hundreds, came when a member couldn't attend a scheduled speech by a prominent national figure, but she told me she was sending the new dean of her local university in her place because he needed to know who we were.

Now and then someone asks what we want in new Prichard Committee members. We are still looking for the same qualities the original members had: (1) an interest in education, (2) a belief that government belongs to us and is not the enemy, and (3) a belief that change is possible and citizens' efforts can make a difference.

The characteristics of the new members also were critical since this was to be a working committee. I designed the work so the group would meet often enough and talk enough to make its own recommendations and fully understand staff-suggested recommendations. Including subcommittees and the full group, there were about 70 meetings over an 18-month period.

Creating an engaged group also meant that volunteer members needed to speak boldly and for themselves. Sacred cows had to be confronted. We wanted to raise the visibility of higher education issues that had been swept under the table for years or, as one journalist liked to say, "throw stink bombs in over the transom." This required volunteer members with self-confidence, fortitude, and values, and staff to offer encouragement and support. All our processes were designed to create these. The committee meetings and their topics were some of the state's hottest news, so there were many opportunities for members to speak for themselves. Chairman Prichard was a regular media source and a spokesman of extraordinary skill. His example motivated others.

Attention to process and to the result—action, not just words—meant fostering deep involvement for our volunteer members. To encourage this, we held our meetings in a retreat setting, usually over a 2-day period. This provided time for both formal and informal interaction, and because of Prichard's magnetism and the personal skills of other members, personal bonds formed easily. Likewise, we were attentive to details such as table arrangements and amenities. Because educators (in this case, university presidents) tend to dominate lay groups like this, they were not asked to be members of the committee. Much to their dismay, they were seated in the audience, not around the table with the volunteers. We also were careful to put members who were skilled at group dynamics, those who fostered openness and full dialogue, in positions at the table or on the program where they could exercise their skills.

The point of worrying so much about process was to make the committee's work serious. Creating an aura of seriousness also meant doing serious intellectual work. The staff's job was to frame issues and lead discussions, provide supportive materials, shape meeting agendas and key questions, schedule outside experts, and draft recommendations and the final report. It became a joke among the volunteers that we deluged them with scholarly articles, news clips, and data; but we were also careful to guide them through these voluminous materials and make them digestible with summary explanations. We brought in as speakers some of the nation's most thoughtful higher education scholars.

For serious people like our volunteer members, real work builds interest and commitment. It makes them realize that they're part of something big, a part of history, and that's the way the committee members came to feel.

To build group solidarity, we also asked our members to use a consensus decision-making process. In 20 months only one vote was taken (whether to recommend closing one of three public law schools). The consensus approach minimized lobbying from outside and made it difficult to kill proposals with parliamentary maneuvers. Consensus building also cemented the group and built cohesiveness around recommendations. As staff, I had the challenge of crafting their discussion into rationales and recommendations that made sense and were based on research or analysis, while making sure that volunteers would see their own ideas when they received the written versions of what they had said.

ENCOURAGING MEDIA ATTENTION

Media attention and confrontations also help build group solidarity. There was plenty of both. Contrary to traditional government practice, we opened all meetings to the media and encouraged reporters' attendance. Because our topic was hot and the state's newspapers had skilled higher education reporters, the committee's ideas and discussions—not just its final recommendations—were fully exposed in the press. Going further, we leaked stories to build interest or to head off opposition. Darkness is a good cover for defensive bureaucrats, making it possible to kill an idea with no fingerprints. Media exposure is the only antidote. A popular suggestion from the committee was likely to generate newspaper editorials and other endorsements before its opponents could attack it or members could be pressured in private to change their minds.

Media exposure also made the work more serious for our volunteers. Prichard's favorite Lord Acton quip, "nothing so concentrates the mind as the prospect of hanging at dawn," translated to me as "nothing so concentrates the mind like the cold eye of a TV camera." Our members were reminded of this every time they met. All meetings were broadcast statewide on educational television. Huge segments were also carried by commercial television.

REACHING EDUCATORS

Since the committee had no professional educators or university presidents as members, we reached out to them in other ways. We wanted to position ourselves as friends of higher education, both because we were and because it was a good political position. To do this, we quickly made it clear that we, as taxpayers, thought higher education was underfunded. We even went so far as to publicly rebuke the governor when he bashed university presidents as "crybabies" when they complained about his budget.

Our goal was to make sure there was no doubt in the higher education community that we were their friends even when we made unpopular recommendations. We reasoned that early exposure of our friendship would build credibility on campuses, buy us time, and make it clear that we were proposing a political bargain—increased funding would be linked to increased quality and results. This strategy, born out of our higher education work, persists as a core operational technique for us to this day.

MAKING RECOMMENDATIONS

In October 1981 the committee's report *In Pursuit of Excellence* was received by the media and much of the public as "a remarkable document, a blueprint for change" ("Building From the Blueprint," June 8, 1982). Another editorial noted that the report was "unlike many others in that it rattles the eyeteeth of political and educational sacred cows" (Parrish, 1990, p. 14).

In the first months that followed the release of the report, it looked like the Council on Higher Education and elected officials might adopt many of the committee's ideas. But, in the end, most sacred cows went untouched as universities supported only those suggestions that were least difficult and most to their liking. The University of Kentucky's president, for example, pushed through a tougher admissions policy, which we recommended and he wanted anyway, and the University of Louisville later followed suit. The Council on Higher Education endorsed our push for Kentucky's first-ever precollege curriculum, and it was written by a task force led by committee members.

The state's political leadership—the governor and legislators—ignored our more controversial recommendations for revamping Kentucky's higher education system, like cutting duplication by closing some of the state's graduate level and professional degree programs or focusing university missions more purposefully. They also rejected what we called the Fund for Excellence, a big pot of money for endowed chairs and merit-based scholarships.

Veteran *Courier-Journal* reporter Richard Wilson acknowledged in 1998 that the committee's report "didn't really go anywhere" when it was released in 1981:

> But if you read the report and look at the recommendations, I'll bet virtually every one of the recommendations has been implemented. It's just taken a lot of time. The committee was a real catalyst. Although it might have taken a number of years to really set the stage for changes in education, I don't think they would have come without [the committee]. (personal communication, June 20, 1998)

Media reaction to the politicians' sellout was swift and vocal. "Once again, Kentucky has looked academic excellence in the eye, and once again it has averted its gaze," was the appraisal of the *Lexington Herald-Leader* editorial staff.

> The governor had pledged himself to the cause of higher education, and then proceeded to damn [it] with faint praise. Some state representatives moved obstacles in its path, while certain senators threw sand in the works on their side of the Capitol—or, in some notable cases, declined to deliver their promised support. (Parrish, 1990, p. 14)

For the committee members, bewilderment at the politicians' betrayal quickly turned to outrage at the continued failure to put Kentucky's future needs ahead of short-term interests: "We were mad as hell and we weren't going to take it anymore," one member said. "Some people hadn't made good on their promises, and we decided we had to fight back." Some committee participants had expressed concerns that their work was not finished. The political stalemate over their recommendations proved they were right. "It was inconceivable that we would not do something," another member said (Parrish, 1990, p. 16).

Their response to politics as usual was predictable, considering the seeds that had been planted. To move ahead, we decided in 1983 to turn the committee into a freestanding, independent nonprofit corporation, "a group of citizens who are not beholden or responsible to any official backing," as Prichard said (Parrish, 1990, p. 16). We also broadened our agenda to include elementary and secondary education, since our work on higher education had made it clear that Kentucky's educational challenges began in the earliest days of a child's schooling.

The times had changed, too. Across the nation, states were focusing on improved elementary and secondary education. The governors in Arkansas and Mississippi had led the national charge, making Kentucky's leadership look even worse by comparison. Meanwhile, the Reagan administration began what would become a flood of reports criticizing American schools when it published *A Nation at Risk.* Our group's attention to the *importance* of better education coincided with its *awareness* of how poorly Kentucky had done with its public schools (e.g., low funding and adult educational attainment among the lowest in the nation).

DECIDING TO CONTINUE

The decision to go forward as a private, independent organization deserves elaboration because that decision has made the Prichard Committee unusual among groups with similar purposes. What led 30 private citizens to volunteer themselves to speak for their fellow citizens? Why did they think that other citizens needed a voice? Why did we go to the trouble of creating a new organization?

1. The education problems were serious. They had existed for decades and had not been attacked aggressively by elected officials. Public trust was at rock bottom. There was little faith that the education community could or would attack the problem alone, especially if it involved threats to the established order. Our volunteers felt that obvious problems had been ignored long enough.

2. We thought educators and officials who wanted to solve problems needed encouragement. This meant that new ideas, a different

view of the problem, and fresh solutions would help. Many educators wanted much more for their students, but they needed support.

3. Politicians were reluctant and cautious and had little political incentive to act boldly. Proposals to reform schools and increase taxes to provide more funding were not popular. There was a stalemate among interest groups. Politicians in the early 1980s gravitated toward the quick and simple solutions, which the U.S. Education Commissioner described as "a mile wide and an inch deep." These shallow solutions—quick responses to pressure—ignored larger systemic educational and social conditions.

4. The public and parents were feeling shut out, believing either that the problem was too complex to understand or that it was too difficult to tackle issues that sounded highly technical and were usually described with incomprehensible jargon. There was a feeling of hopelessness. We began with the idea that almost all parents care deeply about the education of their children, but need help channeling their care. We saw creating hopefulness to replace hopelessness as essential.

5. The volunteers and I all had a sense that we were engaged in something that was bigger than improving schools. As activist citizens, we understood that the complex and intractable problems our state faced, like others across the nation, were not to be solved by government action alone. What was needed was a reinvestment by citizens themselves in their civic capital—in weakened communities, institutions, and social organizations. We believed that the solutions required the mobilization of communities and individuals to solve their own problems. The committee's volunteers were comfortable using skills of citizenship and encouraging others to do the same to get people's attention, to take responsibility, and to send a message to those with legal authority that they must also take action. We believed that Kentucky's problems weren't caused by someone else but were the citizens' own responsibility.

6. We had assembled on the committee people who knew they had a right to express their views, not those who readily deferred to professional expertise, authority, or power. Working together for several years strengthened their already stiff backbones.

If education quality had been the top priority for most Kentucky politicians and voters, Kentucky schools wouldn't have been famous for overall poor performance. Concern about public education had been, to borrow an old Kentucky saying, "sleepy as a dead pig in the sun."

For the committee, the shift in focus from higher education to elementary and secondary education was natural. Knowledgeable people knew that the two were linked. Evidence about the condition of public schools made problems apparent, as did deeply rooted poverty and unemployment. Kentucky was an "unlikely place" for reform, a national news magazine would later report. It was right.

CHAPTER 2

The Heart of It All: Credibility

Who authorized you?

—Kentucky teacher, 1990

The earliest years of life are as critical for organizations as they are for children. How things start makes a difference. I'm reminded of an experience from 1990, just after the passage of the Kentucky Education Reform Act and 10 years after the committee first met to address postsecondary education.

A teacher acquaintance, unhappy with Kentucky's new reforms and holding the Prichard Committee responsible, confronted me at a dinner party. She knew we weren't a government organization. She was visibly angry. She repeated her question again and again: "Who authorized you? Who authorized you?"

LEADING WITHOUT AUTHORITY

The citizen members of the Prichard Committee who volunteered as education advocates would have been surprised at the size of the gap between their own sense of their responsibilities as citizens and the view of this teacher. But her question was fundamental. Many people wonder, Who authorized you? even if they don't ask the question out loud.

The question of authorization is an interesting one. By the time she asked her question, the Prichard Committee was about 12 years old. By then it had achieved substantial credibility, had a committed volunteer membership, and was perceived to have been instrumental in setting the education agenda that led to the passage of Kentucky's school reform in 1990. It was viewed in some circles as a powerful organization. Credibility—being taken seriously—is central to the success of any organization, particularly one with no official status or authorization.

Professor Ronald Heifetz argues that effective leadership mobilizes people to make progress to solve the problems they believe they have. It requires "identifying the adaptive challenge, . . . keeping distress within a productive range, directing attention to ripening issues and not diversions, giving the work back to the people, and protecting voices of leadership in the community" (1994, p. 70). Both authorized (elected or appointed) and nonauthorized (independent, outside) organizations can provide such leadership.

Nonprofit advocacy groups often provide this nonauthorized leadership. But they need to understand what it means to lead without authority. And they need to recognize the power inherent in their informal status. "Formal authorization brings with it the powers of an office, but informal authorization brings with it subtle yet substantial power to extend one's reach way beyond the limits of the job description" writes Heifetz (p. 102). Extending beyond the job description is the central concept. It's also difficult for many people to grasp.

In contrast to governmental and other authorized leadership, and without the burdens of office, citizens' groups have the power to win the public's attention and trust, the power to raise disturbing questions, the power to focus on a single issue, the power to set the pace, and the power to get reliable frontline information.

Without formal authority, citizens' groups like the Prichard Committee volunteer themselves to solve their own or others' problems even though operating without authority is not comfortable for everyone. Once volunteered, these informal authorities can acquire substantial resources, says Heifetz. "Attention, the power to frame issues, and some power to pace the work, to turn up the heat or lower it, . . . power to set the context for action focus attention on the issues that are ripe and important" (1994, p. 219).

Nancy C. Roberts and Paula J. King, in their study of policy entrepreneurs, similarly maintain that

> outsiders . . . are freer to explore beyond existing givens. Limited only in their conceptual ability to envision a new order, they can question tradition and pursue a radical course of action. Thus . . . radical innovation is likely to start with small, unconstrained, close-knit groups working outside the institutional order. (1996, p. 206)

Understanding and using the resources that result from independence is central to organizations like the Prichard Committee. Without formal authority, we undertook to mobilize our fellow citizens and engage them in the processes of change. That decision and the actions that followed from it are central to understanding the Committee. Nonauthorized or outside groups begin with nothing but their ideas and commitments. They start with no credibility. That's why the way they begin their work is so important. It can be the source of their most valuable capital—trust, reputation, and being taken seriously.

TRANSFORMING THE COMMITTEE

The Prichard Committee navigated a critical juncture when it moved from being an authorized organization of a state government council to the nonauthorized status of an independent organization in the early 1980s. Its work to that point had developed volunteers' commitment to getting something done. It also helped them understand that Kentucky's historic educational malnutrition was not limited to higher education. Elementary and secondary education was more deficient than higher education. It was self-evident that education was a seamless web.

By the summer of 1983 the Prichard Committee for Academic Excellence was a different organization—a nonprofit, nonpartisan, volunteer, citizens' advocacy group created to push for improved education at all levels. We added about 30 new members to those who had served on the original higher education panel. Two men who would later be elected governor of the state were asked to join the committee, as were a former governor and many community activists.

The seeds of the Committee's transformation from an official body to a nonauthorized, independent group had been there from the beginning. From the start the members had been personally committed to citizen leadership, a commitment that was reinforced and nurtured by group processes that immersed them deeply in issues and built personal relationships among the members. They were forced to defend their positions in tense public situations. One of my proudest moments was watching a grocery store owner explain and defend a recommendation to close one of the state's three law schools to a roomful of 200 university presidents, legislators, television reporters and cameramen, and spectators. Here was a citizen confidently making the case for a measure that no politician or university president would defend in public.

The group's credibility, established early, gave it access to policy makers and donors. And funding was a critical need. Despite awareness among business executives of the need to improve education, fund-raising was, at the beginning and forever after, difficult. But a private business group did offer a challenge grant. A Louisville foundation, with the encouragement of a committee member who was on its board of directors, awarded a multiyear grant, even though its members were nervous about advocacy work (Parrish, 1990, p. 17). No national foundations were interested. First-year funding of about $100,000 was assembled.

Early credibility also buoyed the Committee's volunteer members so they believed their volunteered time, their most valuable asset, might accomplish something. "Kentucky needs such a non-governmental group on a continuing basis as a monitor of and advocate for its universities," one editorial stated. The work the Committee had started is a "job that isn't finished" ("Building From the Blueprint," 1982).

Obviously luck and chance played a part. But decisions were critical too. These included the decisions about the group's chair, the mix of personalities in the membership (high-profile people plus less-visible activists), group processes that created ownership of recommendations (no rubber stamping), total openness with the media (to gain trust), enough time for deep deliberation (to build confidence and commitment), reaching out to professionals who were not members of the group (for knowledge and credibility), and making recommendations that were intellectually defensible and publicly popular, if not universally acceptable to the education establishment.

PRINCIPLES OF OPERATION

Getting enough credibility to be effective could be seen as encompassing how we did everything—credibility is the whole point. I realized this not long ago when I was asked to speak to a group of business leaders in New Jersey about lessons from the Prichard Committee. My host, a corporate executive, asked if I could focus on what he called the *operating principles* that guided our work. The background materials I had sent to him made it obvious to him that certain values or principles were underlying everything. His question pushed me to think differently. His way of asking what he needed to know was useful when I met with his group, and it may be a useful way to explain our foundational thinking here. So let's think about these principles of operation.

From the Committee's start in the 1980s we knew that we needed to think strategically about the way we operated. We saw ourselves as having certain characteristics that, in retrospect, show where we fit in the public engagement world that is discussed by education reform strategists. Today people often talk about public engagement as if it means that school systems should involve the public as supporters. We were not—we still are not—about that, although support for public schools is a critical element of what we do. So what were the "principles" that led to credibility?

- From the outset, we considered our effort to be more of a *movement* than an organization. Our job, we thought, was to organize the parade and either lead it or find others to lead it, not to create a permanent institution. Leading the parade meant we needed a compelling vision.

- We saw ourselves as a *citizens' voice*. This meant that we spoke as citizens, not as experts. We thought there was great strength in saying, "We are simply concerned taxpayers, concerned parents, and we care a lot about our schools." We tried to avoid the extremes that came to characterize American political debate in the 1980s. When the school reform debate heated up in the early 1990s, we tried to avoid the ideological passions that were inflamed across the country. We tried to stay in the middle of the political spectrum.

Seeing ourselves as a citizen voice also shaped decisions about our membership. We were set up so that the existing members of the Prichard Committee selected new members, a self-perpetuating group without any term limits. As mentioned previously, several of our members were highly visible—former governors (four of them) and business leaders—but we also sought local activists, particularly women. We had substantial business involvement as well, but we never saw ourselves as exclusively a business voice and we were not seen that way by others.

- We believed that *building alliances* was extremely important since we could not do everything ourselves and we wanted to lend our public voice to other kinds of voices. It also was an effective political strategy. We formed alliances with such groups as the Kentucky Chamber of Commerce and the Kentucky Economic Development Corporation, an elite group of CEOs, as well as advocacy groups like

the Kentucky Youth Advocates and educational organizations representing administrators and teachers. Sometimes maintaining those alliances was so important that it affected our policy positions. Although we never totally sacrificed a position, there were some points
we didn't push too hard. Maintaining our alliances was a central operating principle. A friend later told us that we were "at the heart of a
web of relationships." That is just where we wanted to be.

• We believed in the value of public education and we *supported
educators*, and we wanted people to know it. Although we knew this
about ourselves, we also knew that others might assume the worst,
that we were enemies of public educators. We did not want to be seen
as teacher bashers, and we were not. We methodically avoided blaming educators or anyone else. It was important to be positive, not negative, so we focused on solutions more than problems. As taxpayers,
we said that we were willing to spend more money on public education, but we also made demands. If more money was to be spent, we
said, increases in quality had to come with the money. Being supportive of adequate school funding was critical to our credibility with educators.

• We thought it was important to *define the problem* and then
set the agenda around it. This meant that we relied heavily on data
about the condition of public schools in Kentucky. In the 1980s we
were constantly speaking with any audience that would hear us. We
reached thousands of people.

• Driving everything was our belief that we needed to *set the
agenda*. We knew that for this to happen, we had to have a plan of
reform. We didn't have such a plan before we started. Instead, we
wrote it with extensive involvement from our volunteer members,
educators, and experts. We worked in full public view, inviting the
media to every meeting. Once we had agreed upon our plan, we had
leeway to consider topics that were not in it because we could judge
every new measure that came along—whether proposed by a legislator
or originating with some other education group—against our own recommendations.

• The characteristics of our reform agenda and its substance also
helped define other strategies. We talked about issues at the *level of
principle*, not detail, with the goal of setting a general direction. We
dealt with specifics only when necessary. This gave us room to ma-
neuver. We emphasized the importance of teacher quality and improved teacher preparation, for example, but we did not try to tell
colleges of education how to specifically improve. As another example, we emphasized the need for schools to focus on accountability

and high standards but did not specify the kind of accountability that they should use. Instead, we set some guidelines so we would know a good product when we saw it. We reasoned that we would be most credible if we presented ourselves simply as private and concerned citizens, not as experts, and private citizens don't usually indulge in detailed technical solutions.

• We knew that *listening was important* both to get ideas and to build credibility. Not only did we need to be good listeners, but everybody—educators in particular—needed to believe that we were good listeners. We invited educators to our meetings to tell us what they thought. We also asked experts to give us their advice. We recognized that new recruits needed go through the same, sometimes laborious, thinking processes we experienced when we framed our recommendations. Just because one group has spent hours laboring over data and options and reaching agreement does not mean that other people will accept those recommendations. So constant dialogue, rehashing previous dialogues, was essential.

• We also knew that *staying focused* was critical. Academic results were paramount for us. We resisted being diverted into local or technical educational issues, or hot-button social issues such as prayer in the classroom or the distribution of condoms in the schools. Over time, most people accepted this and stopped expecting us to get involved at the local school level. Our job, in our minds, was to deal with the big picture and the vision, not the details, and certainly not local issues or those peripheral to improved student learning.

• We wanted to *confront without being confrontational.* We positioned ourselves as demanding moderates. We lived by the direction of one of Ed Prichard's favorite lines, that our job was to "afflict the comfortable and comfort the afflicted." But we tried to afflict so we could live to fight another day. We knew we had opponents; we didn't need enemies.

• We recognized the importance of *giving lots of credit.* Texas Interfaith founder Ernie Cortez jokes that the first rule of politics is to take credit, shift blame, and look for windows of opportunity. We followed the opposite adage, that you can accomplish a lot by thanking people for things they haven't done yet. We wanted the Prichard Committee to be visible, but it was more important that others, particularly elected politicians, received credit for what they said or did that we liked. We figured we would be successful when others were saying what we wanted them to say. At a recent conference of organizations like ours, someone described this approach as leading with the flashlight pointed ahead instead of on your own face.

- We were comfortable *working behind the scenes*. It was more important that our issues be known to the public than it was that the organization be known. Our objective was to be at the table when policies were discussed. We worked behind the scenes to establish the Kentucky Institute for Education Research and the Kentucky Association of School Councils. We served on task forces and commissions. Ironically, working behind the scenes sometimes led others to think we had more power than we did, especially with the media.

- We saw the *media as our friend* not our enemy. We formed an alliance early with the largest newspapers, meeting with publishers and telling them exactly what we were up to. We invited the press to all of our meetings, and we stayed in regular contact. A huge portion of my time was spent working with the media. We also thought we should provide solid information and be a source of reliable advice. We were completely open. Everything we did was in public. In 1983 and 1984, for instance, I calculated that we had 67 meetings; the press was invited to every one and attended most.

- We wanted to *represent the general population*, folks who cared but who could not be engaged with us or attend meetings day to day. To do this we needed to spend lots of time organizing and reaching out. Our statewide town forum in 1984 (described in Chapter 3) became a symbol of that reaching out. The approach also resulted in the creation of the Commonwealth Institute for Parent Leadership in the 1990s (see Chapter 8). We operated simultaneously both at the policy level and the grassroots level, an intentional way of doing things.

- We lobbied the legislature but thought that the *most effective lobbying would be through others*. We did not have the resources or the skills to match organizations with large staffs, professional lobbyists, and thousands of members, so we used allies in businesses or the chamber of commerce. We hoped that the citizens who agreed with us, and our own volunteers, would lobby informally at home in their communities. We also hoped that newspapers' editorial positions and the news they decided to cover would encourage and support what others, such as corporate lobbyists, were saying.

- We operated on the principle that we had to *speak about the needs of all children, not just the disadvantaged*. We knew from the start that educational malnutrition was most severe for children in the poorest rural and inner-city areas. (About 50% of Kentucky students are economically disadvantaged; about 10% are African American and 1% Latino.) But we tried to speak for all children because we did not think it would be effective strategically to push only for disadvantaged students. After all, we reasoned, mediocrity hurt every child. The middle class needed to get into this movement, we believed, so we needed to show them that they have as much of a stake in the quality of schools as do parents with fewer advantages.

These principles of operation that our New Jersey friend had requested sum up almost everything about the way we have operated and still operate today. With considerable credibility, with a sense of how we wanted to operate as an independent, nonauthorized group, and with a foundation of committed activism on the part of our members, we began our independent advocacy phase.

CHAPTER 3

Defining the Agenda and Getting Attention

We need to have a great welling up from the grassroots of citizen interest, parent interest, teacher interest, even pupil interest.
—Edward Prichard, October 10, 1984

How would Kentucky break with its history of low spending and poor academic results? Our conclusion: Someone had to define the problem, set a new agenda and, in the process, replace Kentuckians' hopelessness with hopefulness.

AGENDA SETTING

The process of setting agendas can be divided into three parts: defining the problem, challenging outdated beliefs, and providing a way out. The agenda-setting process is as important as the product. With skill and luck the agenda may even be adopted as policy. Although the agenda is not the end in itself, its value far exceeds its content.

Once we reorganized in 1983, we began immediately to define where we stood by seeking agreement on recommendations for improving Kentucky education. For our volunteers, the process of agreeing on problems and recommendations contributed to building our capacity, credibility, and effectiveness. Credibility over time comes not just from pointing out problems but from proposing solutions. Later, when some of our initial solutions became the focus of intense public debate in the 1990s, after the passage of the Kentucky Education Reform Act, the seeds we had planted when we formed our own agenda in the 1980s were invaluable. They gave our volunteer citizens ground on which to stand and a vision worth defending.

Sometimes the discussions I hear about public engagement in education sound as if the engagement, or the public dialogue, is an end in itself. We didn't see it that way. In our view, the purpose of an engaged public was to improve public education. With that as our goal, we needed to start with solutions worth fighting for.

As we had found when we were dealing with higher education, the process of reaching agreement on recommendations through study, analysis, reflection, and debate built group solidarity. Four subcommittees of our 70-member group met about 60 times over 2 years. That work drew people together and built familiarity. Consultants visited, bringing new ideas and intellectual stimulation; outside views made the work interesting for folks who enjoyed policy discussions. Consensus building—no votes were taken—built mutual respect, increased regard for complexity and nuance, and fostered suspicion of simplistic quick fixes.

Setting their own reform agenda, with plenty of time to do it, helped our members appreciate the complexity of the problem and the value of having a clear focus. To be effective, hundreds of problems and solutions had to be distilled into a handful of key points.

As noted earlier, we also made an important strategic decision to address topics more at the level of principle than of detail. This decision was both practical and tactical. It was practical because we were parents and citizens, not educators or researchers. It was tactical because it allowed discussions to move forward and not get mired in insolvable dilemmas.

When it came time to promote specific recommendations to legislators or others, recommendations at the level of principle provided flexibility and more easily defensible positions. At this level, for instance, we spoke of improved instruction for all children with adequate resources, teacher training, high standards, and incentives, but did not attempt to decide what classroom teaching methods would be most effective. We never tried to decide, for instance, how to teach reading. Instead, we emphasized the goal that all children should be taught to read well. We proposed universal preschool for 3- and 4-year-olds, but not how to provide it. We argued for increased school funding and increased taxes to achieve it, and we reported which taxes were producing desired revenue and which were not, but we did not recommend that a specific tax should be increased.

The process of refining our thinking was also useful for promoting our views in public, especially to audiences that were suspicious or negative. A leader of the Minneapolis Civic League once told me, "We're a think tank, but the people do the thinking." "Doing the thinking" gives public volunteers the confidence, skills, and knowledge they need to persuade those beyond their small circle. It is practice for the main event—pushing the ideas in larger public forums or in the legislature.

Setting an agenda, if it's done with the public and in open view, also draws attention to new ideas as they flow out through the media like water through an irrigation system. The point is to force ideas into all the fields. Time and publicity is required for that to happen.

We also planned events to call attention to our agenda even as we wrote it. One of these was a high visibility forum we hosted for candidates during a governor's race. Broadcast statewide and well-attended, it gave us the chance to choose themes we wanted to highlight.

We asked educators, politicians, and experts to join in our deliberations as guests. As ideas were floated outward from our meetings in ever expanding circles, the agenda-setting process was a way to engage more and more people. Several hundred people were engaged directly as we wrote our report; others were reached by media. Since our group did not include teachers or school administrators as members, conscious steps were made to listen to their opinions. To reach all teachers, not just the professional organizations, we ran advertisements in 200 newspapers (provided free by the papers) inviting teachers to write with their ideas. About 3,000 responded.

Finally, setting the agenda gave our members their own problem statement and recommendations, published in 1985 as the report *The Path to a Larger Life.* Getting our reform agenda in print was a means, not an end. The end, we believed, was seeing recommendations become reality.

THE MEDIA

In 1982, as we were quietly organizing as a nonprofit organization, the chairman and I met with the publishers and editors of the state's two largest newspapers. The idea was to test their response to the group before we created it and to ask for financial support. The publishers welcomed the creation of the committee, they said, but financial help wasn't possible. They said they would provide something more valuable: ink.

Within weeks, two reporters from one of the papers visited with us. They proposed a 6-month investigation and then a series of feature articles on the condition of Kentucky education. "Was it practical?" they asked. "Would it help?" "What should be covered?" Thus began a quiet cooperation that drew immense attention to Kentucky's educational problems. No amount of volunteer work could have equaled the impact of the six-part, 50,000-word exposé of Kentucky education, complete with recommendations and editorials.

A little later a large competing newspaper, having already committed two full-time reporters to education, started its own special study. They sent reporters to another state, one making national headlines for its education reforms, and related what was happening there to the conditions in Kentucky. Later, the same paper produced a Pulitzer Prize–winning series that exposed gross spending inequities among school districts, misspending, and flagrant favoritism in local tax collection. The series stirred public support for the subsequent 1989 Kentucky Supreme Court ruling on school finance that accelerated the reform effort.

With the state's largest newspapers setting the example, smaller papers followed suit. Several committed full-time reporters to education; one with a circulation of only 40,000 committed two reporters.

Media attention multiplied our impact exponentially. We had only one staff person, so identifying education problems and publicizing them had to be done by others. The media did this. At the same time, regular communication built bonds of trust and mutual helpfulness that lasted for years. Volunteers across the state suggested local citizens as sources of news tips, insights, interviews, background comments, and inside information.

The Committee itself was not the subject of the reporting. Getting attention for the Prichard Committee was not the purpose of working with the media; attention for our issue was the important thing.

CRITICAL ALLIANCES

From the beginning, we built bridges to the business community. On its own the Kentucky Chamber of Commerce had decided that improved elementary and secondary education was a key issue. Because our chairman, Ed Prichard, was so credible and visible, he was appointed to the Chamber's reform commission, and I was asked to help with background work.

Our view was that alliances like this were essential and that cooperation was more productive than competition. We also asked for help from a smaller but more elite and powerful organization composed of the chief executives of Kentucky's 30 largest employers and banks. That group agreed to provide funds, about 25 percent of our small budget. Even more, the executives themselves agreed to make smaller gifts and to support the larger movement with other internal corporate resources. One company, Ashland Inc., began early on to aim its corporate advertising at educational issues and has continued to do so for years.

Our relationship with the media and business was symbiotic. By our presence and our credibility, the committee encouraged others to act. Those actions—tangible support from the media and from business—in turn strengthened the committee, encouraged our volunteer members, and increased our credibility and the perception that we had substantial influence.

REACHING OUT

As the Committee got down to business, we knew we needed to push the message about the desperate need for improved education to other citizens. Kentucky's newly elected governor, a former school teacher, had pledged to make the improvement of education a high priority in her administration. But she also had pledged not to seek tax increases and therefore expected formidable legislative resistance to anything she proposed.

After a legislative defeat in early 1984, the governor was reluctant to present her package again. So we decided to begin the process of engaging and mobilizing the larger public. The idea was to create a public voice to encourage the governor, to provide political cover for friendly legislators, and to expand our own reach by finding sympathetic fellow citizens all across the state.

Our plan was to organize a one-night, statewide town forum of citizens' meetings in every school district in the commonwealth. We knew there was risk. If only a modest number of Kentuckians turned out, it would set back the movement. But the possible gains were greater. If many Kentuckians turned out, school reform could be moved to the next level, and the prospects for a hefty tax increase and comprehensive reform would be brightened.

Our goal was to give as many people as possible a chance to talk, not to write a report or reach consensus. In short, we wanted a crowd. Ed Prichard called volunteers "shock troops in this battle for educational improvements. . . . We need to have a great welling up from the grassroots of citizen interest, parent interest, teacher interest, even pupil interest" ("First Event in Push," 1984, p. A1).

We managed to pull together enough funds to hire a coordinator for the event. She recruited organizers and leaders in each of the state's 176 school districts, and they, in turn, set up planning committees of local volunteers. We worked with a consulting firm to design a highly structured discussion process that would involve people and train facilitators for the local meetings. We wanted to leave nothing to chance.

The project gained momentum, fueled by media interest. There was a growing and somewhat spontaneous enthusiasm. Local folks called to volunteer. School superintendents, feeling that the forum would be useful or that their districts shouldn't be left out, also volunteered.

To give local participants a sense of connection to the whole— thus creating a statewide movement—and to increase attention, we asked Kentucky Educational Television, the statewide educational TV network, to broadcast a welcome from the governor and reports from selected cities. The governor was a Democrat.

All that remained was to ask the governor if she would introduce the forum on a statewide broadcast. In effect, she was agreeing to lead a parade that citizens had already organized and started down the street.

The forums were endorsed by the Kentucky Broadcasters Association, the Kentucky Jaycees, and the Kentucky Press Association, as well as by most of the educational organizations and associations throughout Kentucky. Ashland Inc. agreed to launch a major statewide media campaign with television, radio, and newspaper advertisements, to distribute a million handbills through its statewide network of gas station/convenience stores, and to provide information concerning the meeting sites in each store's market area. Ashland's CEO announced that his corporation believed that the town forums were an "extraordinary approach to get the entire commonwealth involved in the education process" ("Ashland Oil to Promote," 1984, p. C11).

The town forums were scheduled for the evening of November 15, 1984, with a great deal of anticipation and anxiety about the outcome. Many realized that the success or failure of this single event could be a pivotal point for the education reform movement in Kentucky. An editorial opined that "the public response at those meetings will go a long way toward determining whether Kentucky will join such states as Tennessee, Mississippi, North Carolina, Texas, and Florida in a new effort to prepare our children for the future" ("Governor and Legislators," 1984, p. A12).

In the end, 20,000 Kentuckians came together at 145 locations that represented all 176 of the state's school districts. Never before had so many Kentuckians come together to discuss their schools. One paper described the event as "the most massive extravaganza for better schools Kentucky has ever seen" ("State's Town Forums," 1984, p. A12). Another said it "stirred public interest in education in a way that the state had not seen in 75 years" ("Prichard Made Lasting Mark," 1984, p. A12).

About 6,000 citizen comments and suggestions were recorded at the meetings, an additional 1,500 written statements were handed in, and 200 more letters were mailed directly to the Prichard Committee (1985).

Although the committee had no formal authority, many people simply assumed that it did. One newspaper account, for example, referred to the Prichard Committee as "a group appointed by the state to study problems with public education in Kentucky" ("Town Forums Bombarded," 1984, p. A1). A month after the town forums, a Republican state politician declared that "the initiative has been taken away from [the governor] or she let it go, and it's been taken over by the Prichard Committee" ("Collins Says She Accomplished", 1984, pp. A1, A15).

An event as massive and risky as a statewide forum is pivotal for any organization. In this case, the organization had existed for only one year. In retrospect, it was critical to our future.

The governor picked up the movement and led a caravan of dignitaries and celebrities across the state to build more support. She then called a special legislative session to consider her education reform agenda.

The forums were not meant to generate consensus about specific reform recommendations. Instead, we wanted to create a movement by giving many people the chance to speak out, to create a feeling of ownership, and to link people with similar concerns. It also had value as a symbol—a clear statement that many people valued education and wanted it improved in a state that, according to *New York Times* reporter Ted Fiske, "has been content to paddle in the backwaters of American public education" (1990, p. A1).

That so many people turned out, and that the media response was so extraordinary, was a pivotal learning experience for us. The power of inviting people to express their ideas, of providing what some call a safe space for discussion, became apparent. The results also proved to us the power of one group of citizens to motivate other citizens. And they showed that productive and civil conversation was possible. The meetings were highly structured, led by well-trained facilitators who followed a carefully devised plan. They set an example for openness and fairness: All comers were heard, all received responses. The question that we presented for discussion, What do we want for our schools? was written to encourage solutions, not complaints, and to discourage personal attacks on local school officials, teachers, or coaches.

Our forums were trying to build a tent big enough for everybody, so they were designed not to be debates—those could come later. We wanted people to talk and, ideally, to deliberate a little. David Mathews captured the spirit of our forums when he wrote:

> Most political discussions are debates. Charges and countercharges turn politics into a never-ending series of contests. People are swept into taking sides; their energy goes into figuring out whom or what they're for or against. Deliberation is different. It is neither a partisan argument, where opposing sides try to win, nor a casual conversation conducted with civility. It is a vehicle for making tough choices about basic purposes and directions. (1990, pp. 222–223)

The forums also had the side benefit of training almost 400 individuals in the skills they needed to conduct civic and town meetings, skills such as speaking in public, presenting a case, facilitating dialogue, and moderating a meeting. In addition, the committee discovered that it had a network and a mailing list of thousands. What to do next soon became the question.

Across the country in the 1980s events like our forum were usually hosted and organized by governors, legislatures, or educational officials. In most of those events, the sponsors' goal was to generate support for their own reform plans. No doubt many of these served their purpose, usually to arouse a constituency behind a program.

The statewide town forums in Kentucky were different from those in other states because outsiders, a nonauthorized group, sponsored it. And our objective, unlike forums held by many elected officials, was not to promote any specific program. On the contrary, the idea was to listen, to assimilate, and to propose from a mass base. That approach is usually too risky for elected officials.

As we had hoped, many people who took part in the town forums wanted to use their own local event and their assembled volunteers as a launching pad for further efforts. These follow-up meetings would take place, with varying success of course, across the state. One member of the Prichard Committee organized a planning committee in her own county to ensure that a follow-up meeting would be a success, maintaining that the next session constituted the "real test of commitment." She urged her fellow citizens in a public letter to acknowledge that "the schools of [this] county belong to the people of [this] county. They do not stop being our schools because our children graduate, or because we never had any children. If we do not educate our children well, can we escape the consequences? . . . Help us and help our children" (Rosenberg, 1985, p. 2).

Meanwhile, the governor knew she needed greater and more widespread support. Speaking to the Prichard Committee in March 1985, she cautioned that people should "never confuse the support of people in this room . . . with the support we must eventually have to succeed. The plain truth is that many men and women around Kentucky have yet to be persuaded." The governor urged the Prichard Committee to continue its efforts "to create an irresistible momentum" ("Collins Reaffirms," 1985, p. A1, A14).

We agreed to wage a campaign that would involve plain talk about complex issues. The last thing we wanted, one of our members said, was a "blue-ribbon report that's incomprehensible to 98 percent of the public" ("Prichard Panel Says" 1985, p. 5). So we continued.

But something had changed. The afternoon of the town forum, as he was preparing to go to the television studio to open the forum with the governor, Ed Prichard, suffering from poor health for many years, was taken to the hospital. He was in intensive care until he died 6 weeks later. Kentucky lost its most prominent public intellectual and a towering personality. Our volunteers had lost a beloved leader.

Many people, particularly those who knew the Prichard Committee only from a distance, assumed that it would fold. They assumed the group of 70 citizens *was* Ed Prichard. The members themselves, even at Prichard's funeral, assumed the opposite; to them, stopping was not a possibility. Prichard's death, in fact, reenergized them. The vice-chair, a businesswoman and former state League of Women Voters president (and soon to be president of the National League of Women Voters), took on leadership responsibility. A line of other volunteer leaders came forward over the next decade who were widely acknowledged as worthy successors to Ed Prichard. The group had turned another corner.

REACHING CONSENSUS

The town forums actually had been more important for generating attention than for generating ideas. So the 70 citizens on the committee continued to labor over their own recommendations, which they had begun to write in 1983. There were rough similarities between the thinking of the two groups—the Prichard Committee and the collective members of the town forums. But, more important, there was no substantial divergence. This similarity resulted from the focus on broad aspirations and principles and not on finely tuned recommendations. When reforms were actually legislated in 1990, these generalities turned to specifics, and the situation changed dramatically.

As the forums were being organized, the committee continued working on its own report, examining national studies, interviewing teachers and experts, and investigating individual schools and school systems. Most of the recommendations in its report, *The Path to a Larger Life*, were aired before publication because they were widely reported in the press. This tactic, which resulted from inviting reporters to all our meetings, maximized publicity and exposure, kept the issues before the public and politicians, and focused the public's attention on the most important questions.

Our 1985 report covered teachers and the teaching profession; academic goals and curricular matters; issues related to leadership and governance; the need for a new commitment to the welfare and health of children; the need for standards, performance measures, and accountability; adequate school finances; and vocational and community college education.

We asked the public to prepare for a long march, to recognize that effective education reform had to be comprehensive, and comprehensive reform would take decades to devise, pass, and implement. The report concluded that "far too many suggestions have addressed [educational] problems piecemeal" and that the problem as a whole could not be neatly dissected. An integrated plan with fundamental reforms is required" (Prichard Committee, 1987, pp. 1–2).

SUMMING UP

Several things had been accomplished in our first 2 years. We set our own policy direction and our own agenda. Our members had come together as a coherent unit with allegiance to their recommendations, to each other, and to their self-created institution.

We had defined the problem widely via the media, speaking engagements, and the town forum. In our recommendations we concentrated on a few key leverage points for changing schools. But we had also become committed to interconnected sets of actions, to complex solutions, and we had learned not to trust quick fixes. In the process, we sharpened our focus to a few key reform points, a focus we maintained through the coming years.

At the same time, we found in the town forums a successful strategy for drawing larger numbers of people into the conversation. We had "created a public," says historian Tom James (personal communication, November 20, 1994), by giving large numbers of people a chance to talk. With that strategy we heightened public concern, solidified business commitment, expanded our network, and found thousands of others who shared our concerns.

In sum, we had tried to define the terms of the political debate by dramatizing the problems, by defining a set of solutions, and by suggesting a broad political strategy for achieving them politically.

We had established ourselves as an independent group with a focus, an agenda, a network, and credibility. When the group continued after Prichard's death, it became clear to everybody that it was here to stay.

Three core strategies came to drive the work of the group: agenda setting through public study and recommendations; openness with the media to encourage attention to education; and mobilizing the larger public by open forums that were safe places for frustrated people to express themselves.

But another lesson was there as well. Two years of intense effort had not produced legislative action. Nothing had been done that would improve student achievement. It was clear that one big push was not the answer. Commitment over the long run was required.

CHAPTER 4

Blowing On The Embers

Some people are saying the Prichard Committee doesn't know when to quit.
—A state senator, 1985

Following the 1984 town forum, the Prichard Committee gradually found a citizen audience that was larger than the group itself. From the outset we had had a vague sense of what a group like ours, composed of citizens with considerable credibility but limited grassroots visibility and few resources, needed to do. In our original plan (1983) we had agreed on just a few operating principles. We had hoped to start a "massive conversation about Kentucky's educational needs." "Our conversation," we wrote, needs to "tap the well of concern we know is present across Kentucky." We said we needed to "bring parents back into the educational process," and bring "diverse groups together around common concerns" by finding areas of agreement, and avoid "casting blame for the school's problems and ridiculing teachers." This public conversation should "recognize the complexity of the issues and be willing to consider complex solutions," to avoid easy solutions (merit pay, for example), and consider "fundamental restructuring, setting priorities for schools, deciding what was essential, and setting academic expectations and measuring them."

When we described our own work, we spoke of "turning the heat up" and "stirring the pot." This meant pulling together people who were frustrated with their poor local schools and giving them ideas on how to talk about the problem so awareness would take root. The result was a constant back-and-forth interplay: talking to groups of local citizens and encouraging them to talk to one another.

So our goal was to create a public for public schools, borrowing David Mathews' phrase. But doing that seemed overwhelming to an organization with a staff of two and a small budget. The key to success, it turned out, was experimentation: try many strategies and, over time, concentrate on the ones that seemed to work.

PROVIDING DATA

For starters, we needed to show people that Kentucky had a serious education problem and that educational malnutrition paralleled equally dismal economic and social conditions, and to convince them that something could be done if they would help. We began a speaking tour, mailings, press briefings, and everything else we could afford.

"We're citizens and parents like you," we always said, "and we want to talk with you about the problems we all share and about what we can do about them." We printed on several large poster boards data that showed how Kentucky compared to the nation on indicators of educational well-being—high school completion, test scores, college attendance, adult illiteracy, school spending, teacher salaries, and the like. Other posters showed poverty rates, unemployment, welfare dependency, teen pregnancy, out-migration, and health statistics. One poster showed that Kentucky had more counties in extreme poverty than any other state. Another showed high school graduation rates back to 1950 to remind people that Kentucky's low ranking in high school graduates (50th among the states) represented several generations and would take generations to improve.

Although many of the people in our audiences (which numbered thousands over the years) had a personal sense that Kentucky education was inadequate, they were still amazed to see cold lines of data. They didn't know, for instance, that more adults in Kentucky had failed to graduate from high school than in any other state or that more Kentucky children lived in poverty than did children in all but a few other states.

Over time we saw the data on the charts reprinted in newspapers, cited in legislative testimony and speeches, and distributed by parents at school board meetings. Documentation that Kentucky had a genuine problem gradually entered into the mainstream of the everyday thinking of informed people.

MAXIMIZING LOCAL EFFORTS

Under an ideal organizing plan, we would have built an organization from the thousands of people who attended the town forums. Many of the local volunteers who had helped with the forums wanted to keep going. They built on the excitement the forums caused and started local citizens' committees of their own. We had hoped this would happen, but we had little capacity to either serve or control these spontaneous groups.

We worried a little about the element of control. What would happen, we wondered, if a local group using our name struck out in a counterproductive direction, seized a controversial issue that didn't interest us, or embarrassed the Committee? In the end, though, pragmatism prevailed. First, we reasoned that the benefits of spontaneous energy outweighed the dangers. Second, the Committee couldn't control the situation anyway. "Hope for the best" became our operating strategy. And as it turned out, only one local group caused a problem when its local leader began to promote school prayer. When it became clear that the issue wouldn't quietly disappear, several local Prichard Committee members started sitting in on the group's meetings and promoting other topics. Meanwhile, I wrote the local leader and asked that she not use the Committee's name in promoting her issue. She agreed.

Little direct support could be given to these local groups. At most, either I or a volunteer Prichard Committee member might attend a meeting, express support, and help define the problem. Usually, regular phone conversations answered questions or found speakers. The idea was to provide encouragement. But there was no effort and no capacity to train leaders, provide materials, or shape a common agenda. Some skill training was provided through a series of Citizens' Actions Workshops, which concentrated on group process and facilitation skills, but by and large local leaders headed off under their own steam. Still, about 50 local groups, usually naming themselves the Prichard Committee in their town or county, kept plugging away for several years. People took their involvement seriously. They believed they were part of something important. To this day we receive local newspaper obituaries that identify the deceased as members of the Prichard Committee who were actually members of these local groups.

Despite little organizing by us, these groups saw themselves as a movement. Energy grew from within. Even modest attention from our state offices gave the local groups status, and the local groups reinforced the impression that the state Prichard Committee was much bigger than 70 volunteers, two staff, and precious little cash.

"Seeing you do this at the state level tells us we can do it down here," said one volunteer in rural Kentucky. Her comment made me start to realize that above all else we were becoming a symbol of concerned citizens. And being a symbol was something that could be done without massive or sophisticated techniques or campaigns. What we were able to do, coupled with the tone of our messages, was enough to keep our symbolic role alive and growing over time.

Because local training and organizing wasn't possible, we decided that highly visible, albeit limited, statewide efforts were the way to keep local volunteers energized and, at the same time, to push the agenda and define the problem for state officials. Postcard campaigns, press conferences, and newspaper ads were included in this strategy. Our primary objective was to reach out, repeat the message that parents and citizens had a right to express themselves, and show local volunteers that someone was listening. Those messages, in turn, encouraged local organizers in their own, loosely organized, work.

SHARPENING THE FOCUS

As education continued dominating the news and as the Prichard Committee became more visible, we also became more systematic. Local volunteers needed good information about their rights and about local school procedures. One time a citizen called to ask, "Are school board meetings open to the public?" That question stimulated us to publish *The School Answer Book: A Citizens' Guide to Kentucky School Law* (Heine, 1992), written by a part-time staff person and packed with explanations and tips for local activists. About 40,000 copies have been distributed over the years. A newsletter was also started.

Opportunities to make our case grew as public concern about schools increased. Media inquiries came frequently as did opportunities to write opinion pieces for newspapers and trade publications. Television and radio talk shows invited us to be guests. And requests from civic organizations, school groups, and the local ad hoc Prichard groups poured in.

As we talked, we aimed at focusing and shaping the conversation: Poor education was connected to a lagging economy, high poverty, weak civic engagement, and limited opportunities for all Kentuckians. We publicized widely comments by economist David Birch who, in a 1983 speech to the Louisville Rotary Club, had said that Kentucky was headed for "Third World status" because it had the "most poorly educated workforce in America."

Although we could not do all the talking, we did help set the tone. That the Committee kept beating the drum encouraged others to do so too.

As a general rule we continued to focus on general directions and not specifics as we shaped the dialogue. There were several constant themes:

- More money alone won't solve the problem.
- The public will agree to increased taxes if they have faith that academic results will improve. Pay for what's mandated.
- All the conditions that affect children must be addressed, not just classrooms.
- Teachers are the key; they should be supported and encouraged to improve, not blamed.
- Political corruption and nepotism breed inadequacy; they destroy the public's confidence and willingness to invest in schools.
- Cosmetic solutions should be avoided; concentrate on structure, incentives, and accountability for academic achievement.
- Involving the public means opening schools to parents and the broader community.

The challenge came in crafting positions to which citizens would give tacit approval, letting the Prichard Committee advocate on their behalf. Although the broad goal was restructuring the state system of public education, the general principles that many people did agree upon included increased spending for schools, a fairer system of collecting taxes, better teacher training, greater school accountability, and being sure young children were ready for school when they started.

This was a campaign, after all, and using the right rhetoric was important. Staying at the level of inspiration let us build a tent big enough to hold all the interests. As former Governor Bert Combs was fond of saying, "People don't have to agree with everything you propose, they just have to acquiesce"; so we weren't seeking consensus from the entire public.

Later on, specific reform measures in Kentucky's 1990 plan for restructuring public schools would become a problem for many people. With the passage of the Kentucky Education Reform Act in 1990, citizens finally had to confront the details. But in the early stage, we were still operating at the level of abstraction and principle.

I believe we were doing what Ronald A. Heifetz refers to as setting the pace and defining the issues. "Leadership . . . means engaging people to make progress on the adaptive issues they face," Heifetz writes in *Leadership Without Easy Answers*. "Leading without authority" is sometimes an advantageous position.

Instead of providing answers that soothe, one can more readily raise questions that disturb. One does not have to keep the ship on an even keel. One has more *latitude for creative deviance*. Second, leading without or beyond one's authority permits focusing hard on a single issue. One does not have to contend so fully with meeting the multiple expectations of multiple constituencies and providing the holding environment for everybody. One can have an *issue focus*. Third, operating with little or no authority places one closer to the detailed experiences of some of the stakeholders in the situation. One may lose the larger perspective but gain the fine grain of people's hopes, pains, values, habits, and history. One has *frontline information*. (1994, p. 188)

As we talked about reforms in general terms, we built in room for compromise when officials devised specific solutions. But we reserved the right to establish the bottom line: Does the policy support the greater goal of reducing child poverty, improving teacher quality, eliminating political corruption, or raising student achievement?

ENTERING THE POLITICAL ARENA

Meanwhile the political wheels kept turning. Legislative committees met; we testified. Summits were convened by governors; we presented our views. Task forces were appointed; we volunteered to serve.

We spent much time working behind the scenes with legislators. For instance, in 1985 we invited a small group of legislators, all committee chairs, to a private dinner to talk with a national educational reform advocate. They spent four hours debating reform topics. What will merit pay do? Why won't it do what we want? What's the purpose of decentralizing authority to schools? What will change teacher education? What's the best role for local school superintendents and local boards? What is this "systemic reform" we're hearing about?

Following their dinner, the legislators established a special subcommittee on school restructuring. Speakers were invited. Legislative staff reviewed key articles. Legislators traveled to other districts like Rochester (NY), Miami (FL), and Hammond (IN) and to bellwether states like Mississippi and Tennessee. We had been the catalyst. No amount of lobbying could have done as much as that private dinner conversation with a person whose opinions they valued.

We also used gubernatorial races to keep education on the front burner. We arranged a debate among six candidates for governor, broadcast statewide by Kentucky Educational Television. The debate, a common format today but unusual in 1987, generated vast amounts of media attention for the Prichard Committee and for the candidates. One candidate, the eventual winner, floated his idea for a lottery at the forum and attracted massive media attention. And a mistake that night by another candidate, some analysts thought, cost him the election. The candidates' debate was a major political event.

For us these candidate forums did more than solicit the candidates' opinions. They showed that education was important. Our choice of questions allowed us to shape the agenda by deciding what was to be discussed. For example, Kentucky is among the lowest states in the nation in education spending—What will you do about that? is a different question from Will you increase taxes? We knew never to ask questions that would push candidates to make premature decisions or decisions we didn't want them to make.

The debate also gave us a chance to meet privately with candidates and their staffs as they prepared themselves. Those conversations were usually wide-ranging discussions of educational issues and offered a chance to discuss and test ideas. Although we did not endorse candidates, the media would ask us for comments on their positions. Candidates wanted our goodwill.

Finally, the debate was a special event for committee members and citizen allies. It was fun, it was important to be present, and it served to build solidarity and enthusiasm.

DEFINING THE POLICY AGENDA

We also used our own high-visibility gatherings to define the policy agenda. At our 1987 annual meeting our chairman, a health care executive, presented a carefully worded speech saying he was alarmed that education was in danger of being passed over by politicians. Headlines across the state picked up the alarm; editorial writers followed suit.

Education did not slip to the back burner. The governor elected in 1987 came forward with an aggressive and comprehensive reform program, but it quickly became bogged down in political fights with the legislature. With the governor and legislature at odds, quick action did not seem possible.

Yet it was clear that politicians and the public agreed that the education problem must be addressed. This meant our effort to shape solutions became more important. Defining the problem and shaping the solution had, until this time, been both a public activity and a private activity. Groups of citizens met and discussed. Private legislative meetings and conversations with candidates paralleled grassroots discussions.

FORMING A COALITION

But another, much more powerful, strategy was also used, namely, bringing together education groups with differing views to forge consensus. Educational deficiency was an acknowledged problem and educational interest groups shared the public's concern. Some wanted to seize the chance to make gains on long-standing problems such as inadequate local property tax collection. Others, believing that reform was inevitable, wanted to be at the table. It looked like the train might leave the station, and educators were anxious about its destination.

From this atmosphere grew an informal coalition of 10 education interest groups and the Kentucky Department of Education staff. We enthusiastically joined in and recommended that the Kentucky Chamber of Commerce, a powerful and like-minded ally, also be included.

This coalition became a top priority for us. It met almost 60 times between 1987 and 1989 as it hammered out a consensus position. An early decision was made that the group would meet in private to promote open exchange and avoid posturing, and to operate by consensus with an outside facilitator. It was almost invisible to the media. Issues were discussed and recommendations rewritten until there was an agreement, no matter how long it took. Topics where deadlock was inevitable were set aside. The group was completely informal: No corporate structure, bylaws, or officers were created. On the other hand, strict informal rules applied. Everyone would stay at the table; leaving the conversation would be prima facie evidence of disinterest in improved education, each group realized.

A remarkable consensus emerged from those meetings. Rough agreement was reached on general values: decentralizing decision making, setting high academic standards, limiting political abuses, and increasing academic rigor for teachers. There was even general consensus that accountability was acceptable. A rough bargain was struck: Educators would agree to being accountable for improved learning results in return for adequate financial support from the public.

Trust, if not total agreement, was the primary result of the hours that coalition members spent debating issues. That, coupled with a rough agreement among the education community and outsiders like the Prichard Committee and Chamber of Commerce, was invaluable when the legislature took up its own reform package in 1990.

Susan Fuhrman (1994) has observed that independent organizations can help bridge diffuse decision making and moderate dissension among many interests and agencies. Our experience substantiates that. These interest group discussions were influenced by the presence of our outsider citizens' voice, one that was not allied to teachers, superintendents, or board members. That voice helped pull divergent views closer to middle ground. It is also certain that the presence of the Prichard Committee and the Chamber of Commerce raised the stakes for other participants.

MOVING AHEAD

In 1989 the Kentucky Supreme Court declared Kentucky's school system unconstitutional, opening the door for the 1990 Education Reform Act. This presented a different set of challenges for a citizens' lobby like the Prichard Committee. But as the page was turned, several things were clear.

The Prichard Committee had become a symbol for thousands of citizens who were deeply frustrated by their public schools. A sense of public responsibility helped members of the group, who had volunteered for what they thought was temporary duty, become more committed over time. If any of the volunteers had questions about who had "authorized" them, their personal experiences offered clear answers.

They had sent the signal that they were willing to act politically, that they would use their power, and that they would persist. That signal meant they had to be reckoned with in political calculations. Building on our initial credibility, we came to operate comfortably at the community level and at the policy level. We had pulled people together and encouraged them to reassert their citizens' voice, thus building grassroots credibility. Meanwhile, we had defined the problem and the rough framework for a solution, showing that as citizens, not educators, we could be effective with policy as well.

The public was concerned. Opinion polls showed education to be the top public issue. In several polls, strong pluralities even said they would support tax increases. The Prichard Committee provided coherence for that concern and even came to symbolize it. As an institution, the Committee could act and speak. When the media needed a public response, the Committee was available. When public testimony was needed, the Committee was available. When a task force needed a citizen representative, the Committee found a good member. When political candidates needed to be pressed or a school board pushed, a Committee member made a phone call. When a balanced view was needed, the Committee was close at hand. Although the actual membership was small, there was enough genuine and open engagement to legitimize it as a voice for a larger population.

Discussions about engaging the public in public education often stumble on questions about how the "whole" public can be engaged; how every view is to be incorporated; how total consensus is to be reached. Our thinking about engagement in the 1980s was different. We felt that, as citizens, we had seated ourselves at the public table and had started a conversation. We then invited others to join us. Plenty of people knew the conversation was under way. Over a period of years, people could choose to participate or not to participate. Those who did not participate, in our view, had voted with their feet; they had left the decisions to others.

Engagement can mean different things to different people. For the deeply engaged members of the committee, it meant numerous meetings, debating issues, and issuing recommendations in a highly visible manner. For the larger concerned but less engaged public, it meant town forums that could not in a practical way do the same detailed work as a smaller body.

In shaping our strategies we speculated that one cause of public frustration—and thus a way to grab the larger public's attention—was that parents felt shut out of their own schools and isolated from school bureaucracies. We positioned ourselves to respond to that frustration by offering a way for people to feel more comfortable, in the company of a more powerful ally, to reassert themselves in their local schools.

A friend thus speculated that what was done, without foresight, was granting permission for people to do what they already wanted to do. Having granted that permission, we helped people learn and practice the citizenship skills they needed to be effective.

Years later, Uri Treisman observed that the Prichard Committee had become a "centrist" force (personal communication, October 12, 1994). Tom James, a New York University education historian, likewise told me that

> in the policy arena you have groups that are all politics and
> no research (such as ideological groups) or all research and no
> politics (such as academic departments). But you need an or-

ganization that is both policy and politics, based on research, in the middle, that can do both. The Prichard Committee is unique in that it can do both. It sits in places where research and politics meet. (personal communication, November 20, 1994)

We had done this by purposefully pulling people together and encouraging them to voice their frustrations and hopes. At the same time we had used analysis and information to define the problem and show how serious it was. Gradually, alarm about the problem was equaled in the Committee's rhetoric by broad solutions. Focus on solutions at the level of principle was the only practical way to forge a coherent public consensus. Soon, consensus would be tested.

CHAPTER 5

Everything Changes: The Kentucky Education Reform Act

*That kind of creative thinking is government's best role in educa-
tion—setting goals, providing incentives, and then demanding accountability.*

—President George Bush, April 1990

The *New York Times* took notice of the legislature's final vote on
the Kentucky Education Reform Act in a front-page article on March
30, 1990:

The Kentucky General Assembly voted yesterday to abolish its system of
financing and operating the state's 1,500 public schools and to substitute
an entirely new philosophy and structure of management.... While
other states have faced court orders to overhaul their systems of financing
schools to close the gap between rich and poor districts, and some have
sought to improve educational quality through steps like decentralizing
the management of school systems, Kentucky is the first to address both
in a comprehensive package. (Fiske, 1990, p. A1)

A week later, President George Bush praised Kentucky lawmakers
for developing a model school-restructuring plan. "In Kentucky, an
entirely new philosophy of management is being put into place which
is based on . . . accountability," he said. "That kind of creative thinking is government's best role in education—setting goals, providing
incentives, and then demanding accountability" ("Bush Lauds," 1990,
p. 1).

Albert Shanker, president of the American Federation of Teachers, called Kentucky's legislation "the most intelligent state reform program that has been adopted anywhere in the country" (Parrish, 1990, p. 44). *Education Week* referred to the law as "one of the most comprehensive restructuring efforts ever undertaken by a legislature" (Walker, 1990, p. 1).

The details of Kentucky's school transformation plan spread quickly to newspaper readers and television viewers across the country. Within 3 years every major national media outlet had been to Kentucky to document the state's plan to transform its public schools. Some of the attention said as much about where Kentucky had been— and the state's image—as it did about the reforms. "No Place to Go But Up," was the headline on *Education Week*'s feature story (Harp, 1997, p. 114). Noted *Business Week*, "These are important lessons from an unlikely place" ("Kentucky's Class Act," 1997, p. 91).

AN UNBELIEVABLE ACHIEVEMENT

For Prichard Committee members, the Kentucky Education Reform Act (KERA) represented an achievement of almost unbelievable proportions. The decade-long march had finally given us a legislative victory beyond what anyone would have expected. The reform law incorporated some of the major recommendations we and our allies espoused:

- A focus on high achievement for all students
- A system of accountability to increase academic achievement
- Antinepotism policies for school boards and superintendents
- Measures to ensure property would be taxed at its full market value for schools
- A state commissioner of education hired by the state school board, not elected
- Local control given to school councils comprised of educators and parents
- Preschool for disadvantaged children
- Family Resource/Youth Services Centers at high-poverty schools to work past some of the outside barriers to learning
- Vastly increased and more equitable school funding

THE LAWSUIT

In 1989, responding to a lawsuit brought by former Governor Bert Combs for 66 poorly funded school districts seeking financial equity, the Kentucky Supreme Court had declared the state's system of common schools to be unconstitutional and ordered the legislature to rebuild it within a year. "Lest there be any doubt," wrote Chief Justice Robert Stephens, "the result of our decision is that Kentucky's entire system of common schools is unconstitutional. This decision applies to the entire sweep of the system—all its parts and parcels" (Stephens, 1989, p. 66). Years later, *Education Week's Quality Counts* reported that the court's decision still stood as a legal landmark; "no other state has started over from scratch like Kentucky" (Harp, 1997, p. 114).

People often think Kentucky's reform came about because of this decision. It wasn't that simple. No doubt, the decision broke everything loose. It made legislation and a tax increase possible. On the other hand, the decision came on the heels of 6 years of intense public agitation. That civic pressure, I believe, created a climate favorable to such a court decision, and it encouraged the legislature to react in a positive way rather than fight the decision as other state legislatures had.

We played a small role in the actual legal proceedings that resulted in the 1989 decision, although lead plaintiff attorney Bert Combs (a Prichard Committee member) credited the committee's behind the scenes work as being critical to the lawsuit's success. I was an expert witness, using the same data charts I had carried to every chicken dinner I could find across the state. We also filed a friend of the court brief in support of the plaintiffs, claiming that reforms, not just funding equity, were needed to ensure academic equity and adequacy. Political scientist Michael Paris found Kentucky's combination of legal and political advocacy unique, breaking new ground for other legal advocates. The Campaign for Fiscal Equity (CFE), for example, has combined the two strategies in New York.

RETHINKING THE ROLE OF THE COMMITTEE

In 1990 it seemed that the Prichard Committee's perseverance in informing and mobilizing citizens for school reform had paid off. Instead of sticking to financial issues, the Supreme Court had issued a mandate for comprehensive school reforms. The public was aware of the problems. Leaders of the Kentucky General Assembly and Governor Wallace Wilkinson, believing they had citizen backing, outlined a far-reaching plan and supported a tax increase to fund it. The governor signed the bill that authorized $1.27 billion in additional revenues for the 1990–92 biennium, including large budget increases for elementary and secondary education, higher education, and vocational education, plus funding for local projects to sweeten the deal for legislators.

The passage of the reform changed everything for the Prichard Committee. After recovering from the initial euphoria, we quickly returned to earth. We were like the dog that caught the cart: what now? Our original goal was to set the agenda for school reform. What happens when you succeed in getting the agenda adopted? Should we declare victory and retire from the field?

We knew, of course, that it was pointless to advocate for something unless we were willing to defend it. So it seemed to be foreordained that the Prichard Committee would continue after the reform law passed, working to counter inertia or resistance that could be expected to emerge once the full impact of reform was understood. Several years earlier, a state senator remarked to me, "Some people are saying that the Prichard Committee doesn't know when to quit."

Maybe he was right, but he reminded me of the message from George Washington Pluckett of Tammany Hall, who had described reformers, whom he did not admire, as "morning glories, who look lovely in the morning and withered up in a short time, while the regular machines kept on flourishin' forever like fine old oaks" (Riordon, 1963, p. 17). The "fine old oaks" were still standing in Kentucky after the reform bill was signed. One of our members used a different image at one of our meetings: "The dragons are back in their caves, but they'll be out again."

But there was enough logic in the notion that we should declare victory and leave the scene that we had to think through our next steps. It was time to regroup. Citizen members of the Committee had volunteered to push for improvements to the state's public schools. Now that the reforms were on the books, some of our volunteers cautioned that they might be in danger of making the mistake of staying around too long after they had accomplished their goals. If nothing else, we had always struggled to raise enough money to support our small, two-person staff and everybody was tired of that.

In a letter to Committee members seeking advice about the group's future, the board chair suggested that it would be perfectly honorable to celebrate the victory and disband. Perhaps, he suggested, the Prichard Committee should "pass into the sunset" having fulfilled its mission. "What did the volunteer members think?" he asked.

In overwhelming numbers, however, our volunteers disagreed. Passing the education reform law had not solved the problem of ineffective schools, they said. Someone, or some respected institution, needed to monitor the law's implementation. At the heart of this message was their belief that the Prichard Committee had become the most visible sign of a movement in public activism demanding accountability. And as the movement's chief rabble-rousers, these volunteers were not ready to put away their bullhorns and retreat.

"I believe that the Prichard Committee is largely responsible for the heightened awareness of the state of education in Kentucky and the need for significant reforms," one member wrote. "Thus to even consider going out of existence is unconscionable and would be a repudiation of the substantial efforts of hundreds of volunteers and donors. We have engaged the enemy, ignorance and apathy, but we have by no means conquered it."

Why should we conclude, members asked, that passing legislation was the same thing as changing schools? Are we to believe, naively, that educators will simply do what the legislation requires? As one of our members, the Kentucky historian laureate Thomas D. Clark said, "It will be harder to get this into classrooms than it was to pass the legislation." Shouldn't we expect a backlash and a move to repeal the legislation? And what makes us think the public, which screamed for better schools, will either understand or endorse all these changes?

The general public, after all, had supported educational improvement in a general sense. It had never considered or agreed upon the details. Now a specific set of school reform plans was in place, but questions remained:

- Would parents accept the idea that multiage primary classrooms and a novel grading system were best for young children?
- What would new strategies for assessment and accountability mean for educators and students?
- Would school boards abide by antinepotism provisions and remove their relatives from the school system payroll?
- Would boards cooperate with school-based decision making?
- Would there be an antitax backlash?

Members concluded that these challenges almost demanded that a group with the Prichard Committee's reputation for credibility and tenacity stay involved.

"As I see it, the revolution has only just begun," wrote a physician who was on the committee.

We have been its idealistic proponents from the start, but we are faced with an idea borne into a world that is barely familiar with it. I believe the Committee is faced with the unique opportunity of being a role model for a new level of the public's involvement in the education of our children. . . . Ultimately, I believe we're talking about continually increasing our investment in the civic capital of our state.

REVISING OUR STRATEGIES

The decision to stay together and monitor the Kentucky Education Reform Act's implementation represented a significant shift in our original agenda, from pursuing school reform in the abstract to supporting a specific set of strategies for change. We were entering a new frontier of public engagement in education. As citizens, were we going to have to create an enabling environment for reform at the same time we recommended further improvements or adjustments? The Prichard Committee was moving "from the politics of drama to the politics of endurance," to borrow a journalist's description of Eastern Europe's transition to democracy, a phrase that aptly describes the work of the Prichard Committee throughout the 1990s.

We fit into a different place in the education landscape. Symbolizing this was a call I received in 1996 from Kentucky's education commissioner, who told me that the reform act was a finalist in the Ford Foundation/Kennedy School of Government Innovations in Government Award competition. "Could you go to Washington," he asked, "and represent the state and present Kentucky's case?" I agreed to do this, and the reform won the equivalent of a Pulitzer Prize in the government field. The invitation to a citizens' group to represent the state, and winning the award, captured for me the significance of our years-long investment in building credible citizen engagement.

Obtaining reform and sustaining reform require different strategies. But as we searched for new bearings, evolving from agitator to advocate, we also faced a shifting political climate. Just as proponents of better schools had waged a vocal campaign before the reforms were enacted, opponents of reforms emerged to decry the improvement effort as a hazardous experiment. Our advocacy put the Prichard Committee in their sights at the same time political behavior was becoming more polarized and rancorous.

When we decided to continue, we were, in effect, refining our definition of success from passing a school reform law to improving the state's schools. This is a narrow distinction but an important one. Short-term public-issue campaigns come and go, as do "reforms of the month" in schools. By repositioning ourselves to accept a larger and more permanent role in Kentucky's educational transformation, our volunteers agreed to accept responsibility for sustaining the cause they had championed.

"New programs, restructuring of schools, and enhanced finances are not enough, they alone will not provide the means for true educational reform," our internal report concluded as it recommended the Prichard Committee's continuation.

> We must change attitudes, spur involvement, and set new expectations for our schools. . . . To stop now is to deny the truth we have learned through our study of Kentucky's needs. We have been in existence for 10 years now and have seen some success, but such success is only a whit of what we need, what we should expect, and what we must see blossom in this state. (Prichard Committee, 1990, pp. 2–3)

We also needed to find ways to remind people why the reforms, which would be difficult and controversial, were worth the effort. Some of the best advice I received shortly after the reforms were passed by the legislature came from Education Commission of the States President Frank Newman. "Always remember," he told me, "that you may have passed a massive solution for a problem people don't know they have."

Over the next few months, we hammered out a 6-year strategic plan, paralleling the 6-year implementation schedule of the reform law. The plan involved repositioning ourselves and recasting our rhetoric. Through this planning process we came to understand an important characteristic of effective public interest groups—the ability to be flexible as issues emerge. We had no recipe to follow; the science of muddling through by educated guesses and a practical disposition took over.

If there's a golden rule for groups like ours, it's in the words of Stephen Walt:

> The more complex the system and the denser the interactions between the parts, the more difficult it is to anticipate the full effects of any action. Because everything is connected to everything else, even our greatest accomplishments will sow the seeds of future problems. Accepting that fact is itself an achievement, however, if it frees us from a fruitless search for "magic bullets" or an unwarranted faith in the perfectibility of human societies. (1998, pp. 131–132)

WHERE'S THE MONEY?

Before we could pursue a revised mission, however, we had to tend to a practical need—money—which we didn't have. On the day the

Kentucky Education Reform Act was passed, the Committee had two and one-half staff members, a budget of about $150,000, and about 70 volunteer members. Each year since 1983 funds had barely trickled in. Sometimes the flow stopped altogether, jeopardizing salaries and rent payments. More than once, a last minute donor had saved the committee before the checks bounced. Day to day, we had more adrenaline than cash.

"For the Prichard Committee to be a part of Kentucky's educational journey, it must be prepared to pay the freight," an internal subcommittee report noted in 1990. "We have paid as we have traveled, but now, while the cupboards are not bare, they are not stocked sufficiently for a journey of this magnitude or duration" (pp. 5–6). In the spring of 1990 this was merely an exhortation.

But things worked out. A little over one year later the committee had a staff of 12 and an annual budget of $650,000. By 2000 we employed 17 people and had a budget of $2 million. This growth in support enabled us to extend our influence, create several subsidiary groups, and tackle key reform implementation on multiple fronts. It also gave the organization an aura of permanence that its early backers never thought possible. What changed the financial picture was the interest of national foundations.

Before 1990, foundations had shown no interest in Kentucky education or the Prichard Committee. The state simply wasn't competitive. It had achieved marginal national status through the reputations of its colleges and universities, but because it was more rural and less populated than many states, Kentucky's problems didn't attract much philanthropic attention outside its borders.

We had, however, maintained contact with several foundations over the years. I served on several national boards and commissions, which kept us visible. As we worked on fund-raising, I sometimes thought of some fatherly advice I had received. As a boy, I often fished Kentucky's lakes with my father, usually baking in an aluminum boat. When the fish weren't biting, fidgeting took over. "You can't catch fish if your line's not in the water," my father would tell me. His words are the cardinal rule of fund-raising (and pretty much everything else).

The Carnegie Corporation of New York became our first national foundation donor in 1990 when it approved a 2-year grant of $250,000, by far the largest donation in our history. This support signaled a new era since it helped us become better known as a national example. Other foundations came forward, led by the Annie E. Casey Foundation. Within months the Committee had been contacted by groups as diverse as the Education Commission of the States, the Business Roundtable, the National Governors Association, and the Children's Defense Fund. People were clamoring for information about Kentucky's school reforms, and we were able to provide it.

On a practical level, the financial assistance from national foundations also gave us a chance to breathe. Instead of having to worry constantly about paying the rent, we could concentrate more time on rallying support for specific school changes. Nonetheless, fund-raising was then and still is a heavy burden and never easy. In subsequent years we obtained grants from other major donors and national foundations that included Ford, BellSouth, Pew, Edna McConnell Clark, Kellogg, UPS, and Knight-Ridder. But it's not overstatement to say that without the Carnegie Corporation's initial gift, the staff and volunteer members of the Prichard Committee would have had to squeeze money, drop by drop, out of Kentucky's donors—a task with little chance of success partly because there weren't enough of them. Instead, the national grants let us think creatively about the future.

"SOMETIMES YOU'RE THE WINDSHIELD, SOMETIMES YOU'RE THE BUG"

Occasionally, I think Kentucky's state song should be changed from Stephen Foster's "My Old Kentucky Home" to Mary Chapin Carpenter's "Sometimes You're the Windshield, Sometimes You're the Bug."

Everything changed with the passage of reform—especially for the Prichard Committee—and it wasn't always for the better. The dynamics of reform implementation dramatically changed the political environment. There was a host of new challenges, many of them unclear at the beginning. Figure 5.1 shows how I explained these conditions in a 1996 presentation to the committee.

In the decade since the Prichard volunteers first began pushing for improvements in Kentucky's schools, education reform had moved beyond an abstract vision, both in Kentucky and across the nation. The public and business community got what it demanded in general terms: serious changes in educational law. But as reformers' theories became statutes, and as statutes became regulations, programs, and practices, and as those programs and practices reached real children in real schools, the uncertainty about the impact of the changes escalated into fear and outright opposition. It's a cliché, but this time it was true "the devil was in the details."

For the Prichard Committee itself, the major challenge was mov-

Figure 5.1. Environmental Changes for the Prichard Committee

Before KERA (pre-1990)	After KERA (post-1990)
School reform unlikely	Reform legislation enacted
Enemy for Prichard Committee: poor schools	No enemy for Prichard Committee; enemy for others: KERA
Public topic: inadequate education	Public topic: Is KERA working?
Public passion and frustration high	Public passion dwindling
Public cynicism growing	Public cynicism full-blown
School reform nonpartisan	School reform partisan
Media supportive	Media mixed and polarizing
Public concern about learning	Public concern about violence, discipline, and basics
Organized opposition minimal	Organized opposition strong
Prichard Committee = "outsider"	Prichard Committee = "insider"
Some educators eager	Some educators tired
Many parents complacent	Many parents confused

ing from railing against the inadequate system as an outsider to something akin to an insider encouraging, monitoring, and constructively criticizing. "Compared to sustaining change, starting change is relatively easy," wrote Phil Schlechty. "That is why there are so many more changes initiated in schools than are sustained. . . . Two things sustain change. One is a leader or leadership group that acts as a change agent; the other is a system or a group of systems that support change" (2001, pp. 39–40).

Our strategies and tactics had to change dramatically. In later chapters we will address many of these in detail. Figure 5.2 shows what I saw in 1996. In a nutshell, before the Kentucky Education Reform Act was passed, the challenge was to demand change and channel frustration into action. After KERA, the challenge was to encourage patience and support for the reform agenda and retain enough credibility to be able to suggest changes in that agenda as needed.

Veteran education reporter Richard Wilson told me: "All the effort of the Prichard Committee over the years really came to a pinnacle

Figure 5.2. Strategy Changes for the Prichard Committee, 1983–1996

Then (pre-1990)	Now (post-1990)
Talk in generalities	Talk in specifics
Propose general solutions	Explain specific solutions
Stir anger and channel it	Counsel patience
Criticize bureaucratic and political inaction	Mix criticism with praise
Criticize and propose solutions	Praise and propose solutions
Be impatient	Buy time

with the development of KERA. . . . Kentuckians will support change, but by God, they better see results." The public conversation had moved from generalities to specifics: real programs, real schools, and real teachers. Before, the common enemy for concerned citizens was the status quo of poor educational performance; after, defenders of that status quo had a specific enemy—the new reform.

CHAPTER 6

Creating an Environment
to Sustain Change

Any jackass can kick a barn down. It takes a carpenter to build one.
—Wade Mountz, Prichard Committee Chair

The fundamental challenge following enactment of the reforms was to make sure they didn't go away before they were given time to work. Advocates, including the Prichard Committee, needed to focus on creating the political stability and public will to stick with the new program while making changes or improvements along the way. Dozens of obstacles stood in the way of creating such an enabling environment for reform.

One overarching challenge for the Prichard Committee itself was the simple force of political gravity. It has been predictable with reform movements throughout time, writes historian James Morone, that "all causes lose force and shed members after they win the prize. The counterrevolutionaries are the ones who get angry and pay their dues" (2003, p. 333). Opponents of the Kentucky reform had no self-doubt about their righteousness; for supporters it was more complicated and nuanced, for there were indeed problems in the reform. Claiming perfection simply was not possible or honest. Navigating this complexity was a constant struggle after reform had been approved by the legislature.

Educators and the public had little trouble understanding and embracing some features of the reform law, such as preschool programs for disadvantaged children and family resource centers, which aimed at reducing the barriers to learning that occur outside of schools. These add-on programs were popular and generally successful; they also didn't require much in the way of deep school change. But it was a different situation with the portions of the reform that required substantive changes in school practice, such as teaching so all students reached higher academic standards, holding schools accountable for ensuring that they do, and improving classroom teaching. Yet, the success of the core reform concept depended upon the interconnections among its various parts. It had to be implemented as a whole.

A COMPREHENSIVE CHALLENGE

The reform law's greatest strength and greatest weakness was its comprehensiveness, the way all of its pieces fit together. Instead of prescribing what was taught and when, the state set high academic standards for all schools and let educators decide how to meet them. But if teachers were to be held accountable for results, the theory went, the state had to remove impediments to their success and also provide them with adequate resources so they could be successful. That meant hiring good administrators, thus confronting nepotism. It meant providing preschool programs for disadvantaged children so they would come to school ready to learn. It meant committing more time and money for staff training and investing in new tools, such as technology. The list goes on and on.

Complexity was a virtue in the reform as a theory of change. But it was also a liability in a society that favors quick fixes over patient progress, and it made Kentucky's model reform brittle. Having so many moving parts increased the likelihood that a breakdown in one would stop the whole machine from working. All the pieces were needed, but this was hard to explain to the public and legislators. The people who wanted to block the reform, however, understood it well.

ORGANIZED OPPOSITION

As time passed, some politicians came to oppose the reforms; so, predictably, the initial political consensus wasn't easily maintained. There was also an ideological dimension to the political climate, consistent with that which emerged across the nation in the 1990s. Some conservative politicians who wanted to dilute state support for public schools in general, or expand their repertoire of issues, capitalized on weak spots. One of the most vocal opponents was a state senator who homeschooled his own children. In the media and legislative hearings, and later in an unsuccessful campaign for Congress, he repeatedly attacked the reform law as a liberal social experiment that had failed to live up to its billing. He found ready outlets for his opinions, thanks to parents confused by the changes and reporters who routinely sought antireform quotes to balance their polarizing stories. These politicians were encouraged by talk radio hosts and groups like the Eagle Forum and Focus on the Family (represented locally by the Family Foundation), which led the antireform bandwagon in Kentucky and in many other states.

Undermining the reform was easy. Our committee chairman once pointedly conveyed that sentiment to an opponent: "Any jackass can kick a barn down," he said, "but it takes a carpenter to build one."

Ed Reidy, the deputy commissioner in charge of the state's testing and accountability system, told me about a time when both he and a state senator who opposed the whole accountability system testified before a legislative subcommittee. The senator knew that the assessment was the weakest link in the reform. Delay or destroy it, and teachers would lose faith that the reform would last; replacing Kentucky's own test with a national norm-referenced test would kill the new accountability system. (The state had built in a series of rewards and sanctions based on schools' progress toward achievement goals.) This time the legislative committee agreed to stick with the Kentucky Department of Education's proposal and reject the senator's revisions. As the two men walked out of the legislative hearing, the senator turned to the assessment official and said, "You won this time. But you have to win every time. I only have to win once."

The incident illustrates how easy it is to undermine complex reforms and how hard it is to advance them. Cracks in the foundation that don't seem to matter in the beginning will eventually cause an entire structure to crumble. For education reform advocates, this presents a serious dilemma. If they have to repeatedly stop and patch the cracks, they won't be able to move to the next level. But if they ignore the damage, they eventually will have to stop anyway and rebuild the foundation. In either case, almost anyone who wants to chill the reform can easily divert the focus from the task at hand and then claim the confusion they caused is a consequence of the "flawed" reform.

INSTRUCTIVE MISSTEPS

We also discovered the power of accidents and missteps. Surprises and missteps are all but guaranteed in implementing reforms. My favorite symbol of disaster was the fiasco over the state spelling bee. In 1993 representatives of the Louisville *Courier-Journal* and the Kentucky Education Association announced that they had decided to cancel the spelling bee, an event the two groups had jointly sponsored for decades. Out of the blue, a spokesperson for the newspaper declared that the spelling bee wasn't needed anymore—it was inconsistent with the goals of the reform law because it promoted competition instead of collaboration and because memorizing words was no longer important. Valuing "collaboration" over "competition" isn't a mainstream view to start with, but in the culture wars atmosphere it sounded like the worst kind of humanistic, feel-good mumbo jumbo the opposition abhorred. Even worse, the cancellation signaled to horrified parents that the already perplexing reforms were destroying one of the most sacred symbols of American education. And one of the most damning criticisms coming from the back-to-basics camp—that spelling was no longer taught in Kentucky schools—had been verified.

For opponents of Kentucky's reforms, the spelling bee blunder was a wonderful weapon. Combined with the influence of educators who told parents that the reform's emphasis on analysis, writing, and applied learning prevented them from teaching spelling, the mugging of the spelling bee confirmed the misperception that the reform had lowered academic standards—the antithesis of what it actually did.

The firestorm over the spelling bee exposed the gap of understanding between what schools used to be and what they were becoming. It also showed how important every little detail was and served as a reminder that, although education reform required people to cope with a series of hard realities, it also forced them to respond to shifting symbols, myths, and misrepresentations of fact.

Another surprise occurrence—this time a bizarre accident—was even worse. A delivery truck carrying completed test books from about 60 schools to New Hampshire for grading burned on a highway in upstate New York. Thousands of tests were destroyed. Immediately, people began speculating, some seriously, about which of the schools involved wanted their tests destroyed. Had they figured out how to torch the truck? More realistically, teachers worried about retesting, and testing officials worried about reconstructing school scores. (A few years later, when the testing company made a mathematical error and public confidence hit rock bottom, the burning truck incident looked trivial.)

RUNNING AGAINST A MYTH

"One of the most draining aspects of change . . . is the seemingly endless need to correct misimpressions, to answer the same questions yet again," Robert Evans writes in *The Human Side of School Change.*

The larger and more complex an innovation is, and the greater the quantity and quality of change it requires of individuals, the greater its potential—but the more difficult it is to implement. . . . When, as with restructuring, the scope and sophistication of such change go far beyond minor modifications, this transition is especially challenging. (1996, pp. 22–28, 63)

It was a natural tendency, fueled by opponents of Kentucky's school reforms, to remind people of "the good old days" when all the children minded their teachers and loved learning. ("If it ain't broke, don't fix it" was a mantra for many.) That was a time, as one letter-to-the-editor writer explained, when "there were no remedial classes at universities because every student with a high school diploma could read well" (Davenport, 1998, A12).

Such a Camelot of learning was a fiction, of course. Kentucky hadn't earned its bottom rankings on key national education indicators by serving all of its students well. (It was 50th in the nation, for instance, in the percentage of adults with a high school education.) Yet in the uproar about the strange new changes in the state's classrooms, people conveniently believed the view that the old ways were a golden age of fine schools. So we had to debunk the myth of the golden era in education, even if it existed only in people's minds.

False memories weren't unique to Kentucky. For example, *Life* magazine asked the question, How good are our schools? twice, first in 1950 and then in 1999, and found that 50 years ago people had the same opinions as today. "We at *Life* were surprised to discover how many of 1999's education issues were being debated by the public five decades ago," the magazine wrote. "Who's right?" they asked.

Former Solicitor General Robert Bork has written flatly that "our system of public education at the primary and secondary level is not performing as well as it did a half century ago." But the truth, it turns out, is far more complicated and interesting. . . . Even if some schools have become worse, whatever education they offer is available to far more kids. In 1950, fewer than one African-American in four finished high school; that number has grown to almost nine in 10. And girls are now encouraged to become anything from soccer champions to space shuttle commanders. (Hirshberg, 1999, pp. 40–41)

As David Tyack and Larry Cuban remind us in *Tinkering Toward Utopia: A Century of Public School Reform*, "Life at the bottom of the social system has been far different from life at the top. Many people who claimed that the educational system has been marching up the ladder of progress paid scant attention to what was happening to the students on the lower rungs" (1995, p. 8). In Kentucky they had been on the lower rungs for generations.

Kentucky's education reforms were designed to elevate children no matter where they stood on the ladder. There were supports built into the law to ensure that such progress occurred. But that ideal suffered in the hands of educators who did not know how to teach so all their students would learn or who doubted that all children can achieve. A 1994 survey by the Kentucky Institute for Education Research found that only 52 percent of principals, 35 percent of teachers, and 40 percent of the general public believed all children can learn "at a relatively high level." The percentage of principals and teachers who believed the state should set high standards of achievement for all children was even lower. (Holland, 1998, p. 49). These opinions had changed by 1999.

DYNAMICS OF A DIFFICULT CLIMATE

In a climate of fear and uncertainty, such doubts added to the difficulty of implementing the state's ambitious model of school change. For us, the political dynamics required a careful balancing act. Our members felt compelled to support the reform they had worked so hard to achieve, yet we did not want to appear so blind to its shortcomings that we would lose our credibility or look like puppets of the new reform-minded state education department. To move a complex agenda forward both educators and the public have to believe that enough progress is being made so they will stick with the program. On the other hand, there will be setbacks and there will be problems. Progress will likely be slow. Political leaders usually aggravate this problem by making overblown promises and leaving the consequences for someone else to clean up. (Goals 2000 is an example.)

But grandiose promises have real consequences. Politicians have raised expectations, so "even if leaders' performance remains steady, the public is disappointed, and its level of satisfaction is bound to drag." Meanwhile, even as "it is difficult to get things done" in today's adversarial media climate, "it is more difficult than ever to be *perceived* to get things done" (Orren, 1997, pp. 104–105). To combat this situation we needed to (1) be realistic about expectations and hope others were too and (2) get out the news when there was progress *but* also let people know when there was bad news.

CRAFTING A NEW APPROACH

The Prichard Committee had moved from being an outsider railing against the system to an insider encouraging, monitoring, and constructively criticizing. Instead of stirring people to action, we tried to help them understand and support what was—or should have been—happening in their local schools. People going through changes need lots of explaining, as John Gardner recognized in his books on leadership. "Explaining sounds too pedestrian to be on a list of leadership tasks, but every leader recognizes it. People want to know what the problem is, why we are being asked to do certain things, why they face so many frustrations" (1990, pp. 17–18).

This was a complicated challenge. If the public stayed angry about education in general, as they had been in the 1980s, they would force another change and not give the reforms time to work. But we also needed intelligent, civil discussions about educational—now "reform"—issues. Having these discussions, in constructive ways, about new forms of student assessment or the new school council responsibilities, for example, is much harder than fuming about topics like incompetent teachers or high dropout rates, as they had in the 1980s.

In addition to the challenges presented by implementing the specifics of the reform, there were some other factors that affected our response and influenced our thinking. There was the challenge of time itself, not a condition unique to Kentucky reform. Without adequate time "to develop complete and coherent policy designs, change behavior, and influence performance," writes Jacob Adams, reforms won't be able to withstand "the inevitable retrenchment of policy commitment." The promise of groups like the Prichard Committee, Adams contends, "is in their ability to lengthen the race and provide time for reforms to take root" (2003, p. 9). It was hard for everybody to truly understand just how long implementing reform would take. Our volunteer group had to wrestle with its own striking new reality: This will never be over; it will go on forever. Schools will never be "fixed"—continuous improvement is the real imperative. More immediately, the time challenge was that the 6 years allowed for reform implementation in the new law was unrealistic.

And what did implementation mean anyway? Did "implementation in 6 years" mean compliance with the law? Yes. Did it mean improved student achievement? Yes. How long before measurable improvements would be visible? we asked. Ten years, 20 years (the law's timetable), or 40 years? (as one gubernatorial candidate said). No matter what the answer, the organizing challenge was for a longer term than volunteer groups usually tolerate.

One researcher's comment helps show just how slow change could be. In 1996, fully 6 years after the Kentucky Education Reform Act was passed, researcher Barbara Neufeld wrote about her many visits to our largest school district. She noted that "central office administrators talked about suddenly becoming fully aware of the connections between the Kentucky Education Reform Act and standards-based reform." Following shockingly low test scores, educators spoke of the wake-up call of these scores and their determination now (6 years late!) "to focus on curriculum, instruction, assessment, and standards reform more broadly." Neufeld continued,

> We heard administrators say that they had done far too little to inform parents and the community about the true nature of KERA and its implications for teaching, learning, and assessment. They suggested that they had not provided principals and teachers with the knowledge and skill they needed to successfully implement KERA. Finally, we heard intimations among central office administrators that it was time for them to make standards-based reform the district's agenda. (1997, p. 2)

SYSTEMIC OBSTACLES FOR SYSTEMIC REFORM

There were other systemic obstacles. It only took a few years of reform implementation to know what engaged citizens were up against. It became clear that making school reform work would be the toughest challenge our generation of Kentuckians would ever face. A few observations explain why.

* *The reform was much bigger than education.* It was a striking social and political action. The Kentucky Education Reform Act was unusual as a long-term and comprehensive solution. Its vision of all children learning at high levels depended upon changing deeply ingrained practices and attitudes of both educators and average citizens. At the start, most daunting for both were the historical sense of hopelessness in a state with so many poorly educated adults, and doubts that everyone should, or could, be well educated.

Its complexity helped make the reform bigger than education. Citizens were not used to complex solutions, as opposed to simple ones. Complex solutions require public patience and involvement. They also require that bureaucracy solve problems and be creative. Edward

Abbey, novelist and environmentalist, wrote that "the purpose and function of government is not to preside over change but to prevent change" (1989, p. 21). Yes, this is hyperbole, but you don't have to be a government basher to know that bureaucracies are not established to change things; their task is to manage what exists.

• *What Kentucky was trying to do ran against the current political grain.* In the 1980s and 1990s citizens across the nation were feeling more and more disconnected from government and politics. They felt that politicians were ignoring the things they cared most about (e.g., jobs, housing, health care, schools, drugs, and family decline). They were tired of being ignored. Many were mad. Pervasive distrust of both politicians and government was the result. The entire notion that government could do anything worthwhile had been attacked for years by political candidates. It was, in short, a tough time to achieve political stability and for government to implement educational change.

• *It's hard to get people's attention; memories are short.* Citizen interest and public energy caused Kentucky's crusade for school reform in the 1980s, but that was old news. Getting and keeping people's attention was never easy, but it seemed to be getting harder. Just how hard it is struck me as I read a newspaper story about voters' attitudes a few days before the 1995 governor's election. When asked who the candidates were, a dental hygienist said, "I haven't gotten to it yet. Between the funnies and O.J., those are the major things I've been reading lately" (Cross, 1995, p. A1). And most people don't even read newspapers.

Attention to detail is also tough for the public. For many people, the reform act and the new taxes were a massive solution for a problem they didn't know much about. Even though the Prichard Committee and the media had been talking about our poor performance for years, we daily encountered those who did not know how Kentucky education compared to the rest of the nation or how important good schools were. We also saw lots of denial, especially from middle-class parents who said, "My school's fine, the others are the problem." Some suburban parents spoke disparagingly of those "other" schools and children, usually meaning rural eastern Kentucky or inner-city schools serving African Americans.

• *The political clock runs faster than the administrative clock.* Changes take time to implement, and quantifiable results are slow to appear, even under good conditions. The political clock runs fast; it's based on 2-year election cycles. Politicians get impatient fast, and so do voters.

• *Effective communications were important—but hard to deliver.* A difficult communications challenge, typical of any big change, existed from the start; it was compounded by the complexity of the reform itself. To be patient, the public needed to have a general commitment to, and understanding of, the big picture. Someone needed to answer the questions, Why are we doing this? and How do these reform pieces fit together? At the same time, people also needed more detailed information about the 28 different reform elements that were bombarding the schools and parents. Ranging from new property tax assessments to school-based decision making, to antinepotism laws, to new academic standards, these details became the lightning rods for educator frustration and political opposition. So the challenge was to provide, simultaneously, information about the big picture (the problem, the vision, and the solution) and about the details (the specific elements of reform).

• *Stumbling blocks were inevitable.* Given the public mood, it was important to prepare people for bumpy spots in the road like the cancelled spelling bee or burning truck. The challenge was to mix realism with encouragement—not standard operating procedure when governments communicate with the people. People don't tolerate much ambiguity from bureaucrats and elected officials; they think it is waffling.

• *Kentucky school reform was not a panacea.* Things get tougher as the policies of reform theories bump up against practical realities and the people who teach in and run the schools. "We're in the process of getting change worked into daily lives," noted one observer. For example, the reform's theory said that teaching practice needed to improve across the board. School councils (the school-based decision-making component of the reform) were expected to take the lead in improving teaching, but they didn't know what to do. Decisions like these require vast know-how, effective leadership, and lots of time. All were in limited supply.

• *Improving student achievement requires aggressive advocacy for children, improved family conditions, and more involved parents.* Working on the reform was a strong reminder that many school problems are embedded in the deeper difficulties of society, especially conditions that shape and misshape children's lives. The goal was all children learning in a state with one of the nation's largest concentrations of poor children.

• *School performance and results were central to improved education.* This roadblock was particularly relevant for a citizens' organization. For the first time, people were supposed to know, when assessment data was published, just how well their schools were doing. With this results orientation comes more accountability, which rested in the law on teachers and administrators. But in reality parents and other citizens share responsibility with teachers. The core idea was to give both the public and teachers good information about school quality. If they had that information, the theory held, they would do something—something would happen. The idea was old-fashioned democratic reliance on an informed public and informed professionals. Easier said than done!

We decided that true accountability was a civic action, and doing it well required civic capacity. This insight determined much of what we did. By *civic capacity* I mean that the core idea behind standards-driven reforms like Kentucky's is that high academic standards and reliable student achievement data is the first and imperative step before school change. Data is provided to educators, parents, and the public. What's supposed to happen then, of course, is improvement in practice, leadership, materials, school structure, resources, or whatever else results in improved student learning.

The concept behind Kentucky's reform and others like it was that teachers alone cannot be expected to be the sole responders to this achievement data. On the contrary, a community—or civic—response was expected too. If achievement data that was distributed and understandable to the public showed a school was doing well, the public should applaud and support the school. If, on the other hand, the community's school was doing poorly, they should press for change.

So the theory of change for standards-based reform is that people will use the data to make something happen and that everybody—not just teachers—need to be part of the solution. But the general public isn't necessarily equipped and ready for their part of the job. (Neither, of course, are teachers, but resources are available to help them; their adequacy is another topic.) The public, including parents, need help in doing this civic work. That's where other citizens such as the Prichard Committee come in. We defined our job as helping other citizens and parents keep the pressure on the educational establishment in a responsible way. This required skills such as understanding the state data; knowing what to expect in their schools and what questions to ask; having a little patience; facilitating civil school discussions; knowing the power of data; and caring about all children, not just your own.

• *Parents and the public get most of their information from teachers.* Reforms were popular with some teachers and unpopular with others. (Opinion polls showed a pretty even split over many years.)

We all knew, though, that disgruntled individuals are usually most vocal. Publicly supporting the reform was not a popular position for teachers to take. But even I was surprised to see how eager teachers were to share their complaints with parents in settings from classroom conferences to grocery store lines, where they told parents about the damage "reform" or "the state" would cause their children (common were the claims that "we can't teach spelling" or "your child won't be able to get into college").

• *The Kentucky Education Reform Act pushed more responsibility and decisions to the local level than ever before.* School-based decision making (required in all 1,350 schools with a few exceptions) created a new context and opportunity for citizen and parent involvement. Each individual school was the unit of improvement—not the district or the state—so the improvement process was truly a local enterprise and school councils had considerable authority to make changes.

There was widespread national consensus that bringing citizens back onto the public stage—as voters, discussants, problem solvers, activists—was both needed and possible at this historic moment. School reform and school-based decision making were part of this movement in Kentucky. We tried to connect our thinking about expanded community involvement and strengthened civic capital with thinking about school reform.

• *The media changed course.* When support for reform was building in the 1980s, the media helped immeasurably by explaining the problems to the public and publicizing possible solutions. The new media environment in the 1990s may have been, when we look back, the most powerful external change affecting groups like the Prichard Committee, particularly when combined with the take-no-prisoners mood of political debate. As Tom Rosenstiel of the Committee of Concerned Journalists wrote: "If the public does not trust the press, it will turn away from public dialogue. . . . The Pew Research Center has found that the number of people who look forward to watching or reading the news has dropped by nearly 40 percent in a dozen years" (1997, p. 3). This condition is important and it will be discussed at length later.

• *Campaigns to block change are easier than campaigns to promote change.* We were in the middle of a campaign, albeit not a partisan one. But defensive campaigns, like the one that the reform's opponents would launch, needed fewer resources and less time because their goal was clear and simple, easily understood by the public and politicians: It was maintaining the norm, protecting the status quo. To persuade legislators, the opponents only needed to show them how they or their constituents would be damaged if they supported change. Defensive campaigns' ready-made agenda helps them make news—comment for reporters—easily. Proponents of change, on the other hand, need more time and resources, because they have to persuade politicians to take more risks and they have to explain to the public and to politicians what the change is and why it's needed.

CONCLUSION

If these were the obstacles, what did we need to do?

Political scientist Michael Paris, in his study of Kentucky reform, notes that the actors "conduct themselves in ways that demonstrate an awareness that something very important is at stake—that they are "making history" and that the situation calls for efforts to rise above narrow self-interests and politics as usual" (2001, p. 635). That mood, he claims, prevailed when reform was passed and carried into the early implementation years.

We had worked hard to nurture that sense of historic moment and hopefulness in a large segment of the concerned public. Our challenge, as time passed, was to keep that spirit alive as original supporters faded away and new priorities replaced education. Maintaining momentum, I believe, is the central challenge of sustaining civic capacity over the long haul.

To make this happen, we needed to engage the rest of the public more deeply in conversation and help people learn for themselves what it means to be well educated today, not yesterday. We needed to counsel patience through work with the media and parents, and nurture public comfort with long-term solutions rather than quick fixes. We needed to engage more people, especially parents, and help communities think about shared responsibility for their children. We tried to provide a bridge of moderation between elected officials and the public, countering polarizing campaign rhetoric when needed to help policy stay on track and to keep things from veering off in the wrong direction.

We were led to the unavoidable conclusion that implementation was more than changing schools; it required whole communities. If schools are to work well, communities need to do their civic business well.

So we saw our role in improving schools as what we might call "community work" with three intertwined priorities:

- Emphasizing the whole community's responsibility for the broad education and well-being of all children
- Offering support to the schools themselves, where reform must be implemented in specific ways, while also keeping track of what the education bureaucracy did
- Reengaging citizens in civic life in a way that galvanizes citizen leadership and creates a healthy political environment

To do these things we hoped that the public will we had helped to create in our early years would hold together while the improvements we had advocated had time to take effect. The new challenge was to do this community work in the world of implementing reform.

CHAPTER 7

Responding to
the New Challenges

KERA was a love-hate deal. If you love it, you don't say much. If you hate it, you say a lot.

—Parent

As we tried to encourage schools to achieve the high standards that were expected and counseled public patience until schools improved, we went back to strategies that had proved their worth through the 1980s. The plan we adopted was to inform the public about the reform law and its implementation, help set the agenda for public discussion as the reforms took effect, mobilize other citizens for action, and empower parents to be effective advocates for all children.

The key strategies for building public will that we had always used—defining the problem, building credibility, getting attention, giving people important work to do, and being flexible—still applied. But each had been changed by circumstances.

The core challenge, researcher Jacob Adams pointed out, was that "effective change can't be orchestrated from the state Capitol." State policy makers can mandate school reform and allocate resources, but they "simply can't mandate individual willingness and effort to change." That success depended on four things:

- Sustained commitment to improvement among those who must carry it out
- The capacity to translate policies into meaningful, practical results

- Clear, timely communications
- Attention to the many challenges that arise as schools attempt to change

Since these prerequisites cannot all be orchestrated from the state capitol, Adams argues, "good school improvement depends on the mobilization of parents' and educators' essential resources: commitment, capacity, and the support of their communities" (J.E. Adams, personal communication, February, 14, 1997).

Over the long run, concerned citizens are the only ones who can insist on substantive change and ensure its continuity. But they can't do it in isolation. There's a tendency to lose interest. They need information, organization, and encouragement. That is, they need a reason to seek improvements, and thus must be kept *informed and inspired.* They need a way to channel their concerns, and thus must have a way to take their message to policy makers and use their collective influence to *shape the agenda.* They need a way to find others who are committed to the same cause, and thus must be able to *mobilize for action.* Finally, *parents need to be engaged* in special ways as a targeted audience.

There is much overlap between these four broad categories; they all feed each other; they are not mutually exclusive. But they do provide a rough organization for describing citizen advocacy for educational reform in Kentucky.

INFORMING THE PUBLIC

All of our work stemmed from the notion that people will act if they have knowledge and understand the problem. People need to know what they're fighting for and why they must persist, and they need to believe success is possible.

Because Kentucky's reforms were so massive and so novel, the stress on teachers, students, and parents was palpable. Educator resistance mounted in direct proportion to the difficulty of the task. Local conditions compounded the challenge of implementing changes in classrooms. Although many educators were ready and eager for reform, their beacons were not bright; they needed encouragement and support. In some cases, the state and local educational bureaucracies were slow to implement the changes or confusing in their directives to educators; in other situations, they acted contrary to legislative intent. Meanwhile, there were always people who distorted information, seeking to sabotage the reform law or pressure the legislature to weaken it.

For all these reasons, there was a need to reach the public directly with useful and accurate information. It was critical, we thought, to keep the vision and the big picture in front of people. The goal was to be sure that as many people as possible knew what was really happening and supposed to be happening in their schools.

Our most hands-on strategy was to rally allies who could build communities of interest, expanding the engaged and informed public at the local level. To do this, we created Community Committees for Education in school districts across the state. In the fall of 1991 we hired a staff person in our Lexington office to handle this outreach; she recruited six part-time "regional coordinators," or local organizers, to work in communities across the state.

Within a year this team had created about 60 community committees that ranged in size from a half dozen people to more than 50 local volunteers. These "keep-the-faith" committees, as David Hornbeck once called them, enabled us to expand the number of people who cared about and were knowledgeable of Kentucky's school reforms. In addition, the community committees were to prod schools and ask tough questions when needed. They might, for instance, encourage parents to run for school councils. Or they might hold public forums to explain ungraded primary classes, new report cards, or test scores. The big challenge was to provide enough information so people would become genuine participants in the reform process, yet not overwhelm them with so much detail that they would quit or go back to being outraged or apathetic.

We were pleased with the early results. But after 5 years, keeping the community committees energized was a challenge. We found in a 1996 evaluation we commissioned from New York University's Institute for Education and Social Policy that half of the 63 groups were inactive or had become one-person operations. Why? For some people, passage of the reform meant that Kentucky had solved the problems, and their interest declined. Others needed a more defined task than we were giving them through the community committee. For others still, hostility from local school officials or reform critics stifled their initiative; these volunteer community leaders hadn't signed up to take the abuse some of them received.

Eventually, we replaced the community committees with a program that involved parents in much more structured local advocacy work. That program, the Commonwealth Institute for Parent Leadership, became our primary means of informing and mobilizing people who had the time and inclination to be heavily involved (more on this follows).

In addition to informing people in person, we used and can recommend various broad-based approaches that are common to many campaigns.

Advertise

Targeted advertisements brought critical publicity and momentum. Before the reform law was passed, we had used a small amount of paid advertising, but it was too expensive for our limited budget. After the law was passed, our business ally, the Partnership for Kentucky School Reform (later called Partnership for Kentucky Schools), initiated a $1.5 million advertising campaign to help explain the changes to the public. But advertising could best concentrate on big themes; finer grained details had to be communicated in other ways.

Work with the Media

Intelligent and balanced media coverage of reform was essential. We thus saw our task as helping reporters understand the complexities of education so they could write about it with depth and objectivity. We gave reporters story ideas, suggested national experts for interviews, distributed national reports, and helped them find data for articles. For many reporters, we were an informal, readily accessible "research bureau" that could put them in touch with current trends, statistics, or sources on deadline.

We made ourselves available to reporters, and we trained everybody on our staff to respond quickly to the media when they were on deadlines. My son once sent me one of those anonymous e-mail nuggets that said, "You get better press if you're smart and witty and return your phone calls than if you don't." That thinking pretty much drove the way we tried to operate. Being totally open and available to the media was essential for building trust. Since the 1980s all our meetings were open to the press, and questions were answered.

These practices required refinement as opposition to the reforms intensified and the media began casting every story as a battle of extremes—"he said–she said" journalism. The complexities of the reforms do not lend themselves to such easily developed stories, but that didn't keep reporters from trying. I remember one television interview that came to an abrupt end when my answer, reflecting those complexities, could not be neatly categorized as either for or against reform by the reporter.

This is not a trivial matter. Complex social problems require deep reflection and careful analysis. And the ability to find solutions comes from consensus, not conflict. By framing the debate about Kentucky's school reform law as a battle of opposites and focusing on tactics instead of content, the news media played into the hands of obstructionists, who would rather have scrapped the entire package than improve it. In this way, both the media and the groups with single-issue agendas reinforced the public's already shortened attention span.

We eventually learned that it was best to take ourselves out of this polarizing cycle by asking reporters who else they planned to call for comments. (That's a fair question to ask, but reporters may not like it.) If the reporters intended to interview only me and leading antireform groups, I declined to comment, figuring it was better not to be the news than to let the media incessantly pit us as the opposite of an extreme position. As an alternative to my comments, we developed a list of national experts whose opinions could be backed up by research and experience, not just political or ideological views. When reporters called, I urged them to interview some of these authorities instead of relying on the Prichard Committee. It was imperative, we reasoned, to retain some aura of public neutrality. Being pigeonholed, we thought, was a worse fate than not being in the news. We learned that if we didn't play the game, neither could others.

Provide Many Sources of Information

We established a resource center of descriptive materials, set up a toll-free telephone line to answer the public's questions about school reform, started a quarterly newsletter, distributed a monthly opinion column to newspapers around the state, and published guidebooks and reports to explain key provisions of the law. We mailed out thousands of information packets in response to questions; we sold and gave away several thousand copies of guides about assessment, primary programs, and school budgets, as well as an annual review of new legislative developments. The 1,500 telephone questions we received in a typical year on our toll-free line told us that average Kentuckians were hungry for clarifications that the Kentucky Department of Education was often slow to provide. Our monthly column, sent to about 200 newspapers, was usually published in about 75 of them.

We also used some free public service advertising, mostly radio spots, to keep the public conversation about school reform at a high level. With greater financial resources from national foundations after 1990, we could also afford to send out mass mailings telling people how to participate in school council elections and describing the new state achievement tests, among other things. Over the years, we produced about 100 informative items. Our mailing list, as time passed, grew to about 15,000 interested people.

Meet with Citizens/Present our Case

Sitting in the office did not get the job done. From 1990 to 2000, the Prichard Committee members and staff made about 2,000 appearances, from large presentations to Rotary Clubs and assorted conferences, to smaller school PTA meetings, Sunday school classes, coffee socials in people's homes, and various commission and committee meetings. No audience was too small. Altogether we drove over a million miles, from one end of the state to the other. These personal appearances were, I believe, the most effective communications strategy. The reforms were so complex and controversial that one-on-one interaction was more powerful than printed materials mailed by a faceless bureaucracy.

Organize Debates and Conferences

By sponsoring public issue debates and candidate forums, the Prichard Committee positioned itself as an interested, but balanced, player in key discussions about school reform. At the same time, we kept education issues on the political agenda by forcing politicians to address the topic in public settings. A good example of this was our public forums for gubernatorial candidates every 4 years. These had high visibility; they were broadcast statewide on educational television with feeds to commercial stations. They also gave us a good reason to meet with candidates and their staffs to brief them on the issues and to gather our volunteers for a special occasion. (As a nonprofit corporation the committee did not participate in partisan races or endorse candidates. We adhered to the spirit and the letter of the law.)

Encourage Research

We decided early that, although independent research on Kentucky's reforms was important, we did not have the resources or the expertise to provide it. However, we could act as a catalyst to make it happen. During the fall of 1992, for example, we organized with the Partnership for Kentucky School Reform a gathering of 15 state and national researchers to discuss critical issues in systemic reform and the following year worked with the National Governors Association to publish a report that grew out of that conference (David, 1993). We also helped the Partnership obtain foundation funding for a major research project on professional development and collaborated in it for years.

Going further, we used our influence with state officials and national foundations to help create the Kentucky Institute for Education Research (KIER), an independent nonprofit organization charged with evaluating the reforms over time and reporting the results.

As we helped establish KIER, we were faced with a tough question: Should the foundation that wanted to fund the research fund the Prichard Committee to do it? We stewed over our answer. Eventually, though, we decided we did not want a major research function. Our rationale says a lot about our sense of strategies. For one thing, we reasoned that managing a research agenda would spread us too thin and take valuable time and attention from our other purposes. Second, we thought it would jeopardize the credibility of the research itself since we were known as advocates for the reform. We decided that an independent research center, credible on its own, would be best.

Encourage Public Conversations

From the beginning, the public was confused about the new language of reform. To grasp the vocabulary—*high standards, group problem solving, continuous learning, critical thinking, authentic assessment, criterion-referenced tests,* and the like—people needed time for conversations with teachers and other parents who could explain what was happening in classrooms and show them what the new language meant.

Focus-group research indicated that individual responses to the state's reforms were generally positive, particularly where parents and teachers had personal experience with the changes. Yet the same research also showed that citizens and teachers differed in their views and expectations.

To combat knee-jerk responses, we tried to organize careful and structured conversations. We created, for example, Parents and Teachers Talking Together (PT3), a facilitated discussion process to help teachers and parents in individual schools move beyond the issues that divide them to find common goals they can mutually support. Over the years we trained hundreds of volunteers to facilitate these discussions. The local focus was important because people had grown accustomed to blaming the state for every school problem instead of taking responsibility for what they could do themselves. Since 1994 more than 7,500 parents and teachers have participated in these discussions.

Promote the Cause, Not the Organization

Over the years organizations from many states have traveled to Kentucky to learn about our public engagement work. Inevitably, visitors will ask, "How should we get more publicity for our organization?" Our response often comes as a surprise. As advocates, you need publicity for your cause, not your organization. Focus on results. Focus on message. If the message is credible, the organization will be credible. It is more important that people know and talk about your goals than about you; this is the opposite of a traditional political campaign where the personality, not the issue, is key, and visibility is imperative.

Public advocacy groups exist to lead campaigns. If the issue succeeds, the group succeeds. Name recognition is not irrelevant, but it's not as important as the issue. Civic leaders, media representatives, and policy makers must know the group and trust its opinions. But for the larger public, the issue, not the organization, must be known and understood.

Increase the Capacity of Other Communicators

For state-level education reform, most of the resources are in the state department of education. I have thus been surprised to see how many of these large agencies around the country have undervalued, underfunded, or understaffed their communications functions. It's common to see writing that is unclear or jargon-ridden, poorly chosen wordings, an inability to keep agency employees on a common message, and little or no communication with teachers and the general public.

One of our key strategies was to encourage the department of education to improve its own communications strategies and skills. This involved bringing in outside expertise (such as professional public relations firms), common planning, and training for staff. Perhaps most important, with our business allies we worked to convince the bureaucracy that communication must be a top priority and must be done well.

Over the years we learned several key lessons about how to inform and educate our fellow citizens:

- *Be flexible.* It is important to make adjustments and scrap what doesn't work. Results matter most. Reliable feedback about ongoing initiatives is essential.
- *Focus.* Public advocacy groups must help other citizens stay focused on long-term objectives. It's very easy to be distracted; good causes abound. It is important to advance one agenda and devote group resources to work that would have that result.
- *Develop a reputation for integrity.* Credibility is critical. If journalists and policy makers trust an advocacy organization, they will seek opinions and advice from its representatives and, in turn, convey those ideas to the public. This requires presenting a balanced viewpoint and being willing to criticize the reform when deserved.
- *Make the campaign personal.* People must see a personal connection to what's happening. Advocacy groups must take pains to use individual cases, not just theories, to explain their agendas. They should think in terms of anecdotes and success stories instead of policies and laws. Nothing is better than hands-on expertise and personal experience.

One of my favorite examples is the "portfolio nights" at schools, often organized by our parent volunteers. From the start, writing portfolios were a novel and mysterious element of reform. All parents don't believe writing is as important as portfolios imply, and some even doubt that writing can be taught. Portfolio scores also count in the schools' academic performance (about 11 percent), but most people don't believe written work can be objectively evaluated. A portfolio night is an event that gives parents hands-on exposure to portfolios and to the student work in them. After a meal at the school, teachers and writing consultants show parents how portfolio pieces are graded and, in the process, how writing can be taught. The keys to the event's success are using real student work and direct personal contact with a teacher.

- *Be strategic about dissemination.* Advocacy groups must carefully choose their targets. It's impossible to reach everyone, but it is reasonable to reach a selected audience. Small numbers of people can have a large impact with the right information and direction.

As we planned our information campaign there was constant tension between strategies that favored large-scale television and radio advertising and those providing more detailed information to smaller numbers of people. Our inclination was toward the targeted approach. Special occasions provide additional opportunities. We celebrated the reform's 10th anniversary, for instance, with a published progress report, extensive media coverage, and about 50 public events.

• *Let the opponents talk.* Everybody needs to talk openly about reforms, but it's particularly important to let the most extreme voices air their complaints publicly. Although a standard political strategy is to deny your opponents a platform, we have found that extremists often hang themselves with their own verbal ropes. The more frequently people hear outrageous rhetoric, the more likely they will be to reject it in favor of a middle ground. For instance, one of the more inflammatory criticisms of Kentucky's reform was that teachers were teaching witchcraft. It was better to have these charges aired in public than circulate underground. How likely was it, the average parent concluded, that a favorite teacher, one seen at the grocery store buying breakfast cereal, was teaching witchcraft?

• *Form alliances.* With limited financial and staff resources, public advocacy groups can be more effective if they stick to a few, well-conceived projects. But by aligning themselves with other organizations, such as a chamber of commerce or a university think tank, they can broaden their influence and expand the perception of power. Our alliances included the Kentucky Chamber of Commerce, the Kentucky Institute for Education Research, the Partnership for Kentucky Schools, numerous university faculty, and several professional education organizations. Our pooled mailing lists created a database of more than 40,000 Kentuckians.

SHAPING THE AGENDA

How and when issues are raised is a critical factor in reform implementation. Kentucky's reform was comprehensive and complex. Adjustments and changes were needed, but it mattered what was changed, how it was changed, and when it was changed. Overload was always a danger; so was moving too quickly with ill-conceived changes. The Prichard Committee wanted to have a seat at the table when adjustments to Kentucky's school reform were made rather than watch from the sidelines as these adjustments unraveled the entire reform.

Sometimes we served as the voice of history, reminding the public and policy makers about the original intent of the law. We also worked, usually behind the scenes, to influence state policy. The goal was to position ourselves as a fair adviser to anyone who would listen. Adjustments to the law would be needed over time, but these refinements had to be carefully crafted and explained. One example is the quality of teaching.

From the 1980s our agenda had emphasized an array of issues related to teaching quality. We had argued for vastly improved teacher preparation, adequate salaries and a more effective pay system (not merit pay but what is now called *differentiated pay*), good working conditions, better professional development, more time for teachers to plan and learn, and much more. The 1990 reform addressed teaching quality in some ways (higher salaries, a professional standards board, improved professional development) but not adequately. In the years immediately after 1990 it wasn't politically feasible to add substantial teaching quality initiatives; the reform policy plate was just too full. Instead, groups like ours and the Partnership for Kentucky Schools concentrated on one part of the puzzle: enhanced professional development.

Over time school achievement data provided proof that good teaching mattered most of all. Our celebration and report at the 10th anniversary in 2000 was the opportunity to move the teaching quality agenda to the front burner. With a grant from the Carnegie Corporation of New York, we began a campaign that included focus-group research, recommendations from a task force, informational mailings, a speaking tour, visits to newspaper editorial boards, and lobbying legislators.

For us the key questions were which topic among many we should push and when we should push it. Moving too early would likely result in defeat due to disinterest and policy overload; if we moved too late, the problem could become insurmountable.

Numerous strategies helped us influence the reform agenda. Many of those discussed earlier apply here as well, but some stand out for their power to shape agendas.

Organize High-Visibility Events

Most organizations use high-visibility events to force issues into the public bloodstream. We're no exception. Our annual meeting, held for 2 days every summer, is our major vehicle, although in the interim our hot issues are circulated by press releases, opinion leader mailings, and strategic calls to education reporters. The meetings are usually well covered by the media; they also attract a host of top state officials as guests, making it the place to be for informal conversation and news gathering.

Planning the meeting focuses on two objectives: (1) revitalizing our volunteer and staff interest and (2) publicizing topics that need attention. Planning around "what the headline will be" also means we have to stay "on message"; we avoid, therefore, other topics that might compete with our top priority.

Teaching quality is a good example: we highlighted it at our annual meeting 3 years in a row. The first year we released a report to set the stage: We said that despite strong improvement in achievement too many schools were moving too slowly and, we argued, evidence from high-performing, high-poverty schools proved that good teaching made the difference. Persuasive national speakers were called in to generate press attention and make the issue important to our members. Principals and teachers from high-performing schools were added to the mix; their words said, in effect, "if we can teach all kids well, so can everybody."

The next year we announced a major foundation grant to build awareness of teaching, invited university provosts to tell us what they were doing to improve teacher education (and by implication show that we would hold them accountable), and announced recommendations from a special task force we created. We also gave legislators who shared our concern a platform at the meeting and thanked them publicly for their leadership, which we hoped would continue.

The third year we repeated the same theme, adding the message that the teacher pay system needed to be reformed and also that additional funds were required—thus putting the tax reform issue on the front pages of the newspapers as well.

We pushed our annual meeting theme relentlessly. In the year following each meeting we featured it in press releases, in our newsletter (circulated to about 15,000 people), and on our Web site; we made it the theme of all public presentations; we delivered reports and recommendations about it to legislators and other decision makers. Picking key issues meant we were narrowing our agenda—focusing relentlessly—because picking issues also meant we had to decide not to highlight other issues. We had no more than two or three priority topics at any one time.

Form Strategic Alliances

In 1991 we helped create the Partnership for Kentucky School Reform, a project of the Business Roundtable, the national organization of 200 chief executive officers. Our own 6-year plan, written in 1990, had called for creating an alliance of business people to support school change. The Partnership met the objective.

In Kentucky a triumvirate of corporate CEOs took the lead: Oz

Nelson, Chief Executive Officer of United Parcel Service (UPS), which was based in Greenwich, Connecticut, but had its largest concentration of employees in Louisville; John Hall, Chief Executive Officer of Ashland Inc., then headquartered in Ashland, Kentucky; and David Jones, Chairman of Humana Inc., the hospital chain and insurance company that he co-founded in Louisville. Nelson, who took the early lead, concluded that an alliance with a credible volunteer group like the Prichard Committee would be more practical and effective than creating a new, freestanding organization. The Prichard Committee agreed, with the corporations' funding, to hire the Partnership staff, share support staff, and provide office space and organizational support. There was, of course, much overlap between the two organizations, but that was a small price to pay for outstanding business leadership.

Through the Partnership, business leaders made a 10-year commitment to support the reform law's implementation by identifying emerging issues and providing timely information to educators and the public. Their strategies included dispatching a dramatically painted school bus—outfitted with easy-to-read literature and interactive displays—to county fairs, festivals, parades, and school parking lots and actively involving other Kentucky employers and employees in school reform. The Partnership also launched a sophisticated and expensive television and radio ad campaign in the early 1990s.

Perhaps the most important function of the Partnership was encouraging, through the example of its business leaders' commitment, the political and educational power structure in Kentucky to maintain a common front. In addition to CEOs, members included the Kentucky Congress of Parents and Teachers; state associations of school board members, teachers, and school administrators; Kentucky Educational Television; and publishers of the state's largest newspapers. The support of some of the state's top business leaders also encouraged smaller companies to stand behind the reforms and pursue specific changes in local schools.

Why were two organizations needed? We reasoned that if people were going to enthusiastically support a cause, they needed real work to do and a personal stake in the outcome. Kentucky's business leaders needed their own organization to lead. They never would have been as excited about a business subsidiary of the Prichard Committee as they were about an organization they created. Besides, it was good for the Prichard Committee to be connected to the high-profile business group, and it added vast resources of power and money.

This strategy of being an incubator also came into play when the

Prichard Committee, in a modest way, helped establish the Kentucky Association of School Councils, a membership group that trained and supported teachers and parents for their new role guiding the instructional and budgetary practices of local schools. The state legislature created the school councils to give teachers, parents, and administrators authority over key education matters. But we were concerned from the start that parents would underestimate the importance of serving in the elected positions and would be unprepared to do so. Our initial strategic plan called for us to recruit and train council members, but as 1,200 schools began to launch councils, we could see that this massive task was beyond us. We decided that there would be greater advantage in helping an independent group get started than in doing the work ourselves. We encouraged the creation of the Kentucky Association of School Councils and have worked closely with them since.

It was also a priority to maintain the informal education coalition that had been established in 1987 (described in Chapter 4). The coalition has continued to meet almost monthly for 16 years. It encourages consensus on divisive issues, promotes information sharing, serves as an early warning system about controversies or problems, and builds communication between organization executives.

The idea behind all of these—the Partnership, the School Council Association, and the coalition—plus much of our day-to-day work was, as a friend said, "to keep everybody connected to everybody else."

Influence the Bureaucracy

It's a mistake to assume that government will focus attention on the most important issues in a reform campaign. It's also not a sure thing that the various official bodies that study, report, and recommend policy—boards, task forces, commissions—often composed of educators, will always have the larger public interest foremost in their priorities. We therefore concluded that if we were to shape the agenda as a citizens' voice we needed regular interaction with the state department of education, the governor's office, and the legislature and legislative staff. We also needed to have a presence on numerous decision-making bodies, such as the state board of education.

Because we considered parent involvement crucial to school improvement, we worked to make sure state task forces and advisory committees routinely included parent representatives. There was also the matter of contending with the state educational bureaucracy when it came to setting a new agenda and seeing it followed out. During the early 1990s, the process of redesigning the state education bureaucracy had only begun. The Kentucky reform law made a good start by requiring the state department of education to disband and hire or rehire the best employees. A key concept in the reform was that the department would become a service agency instead of an enforcement organization, but employees were caught up in old customs and patterns. Even though the reform pushed decisions to the local level, some state officials still tried to provide—and many local educators demanded—the answer to every question about the reform law's implementation. Some educators continued to play the game of calling state officials until they finally received the interpretation they wanted.

It is much easier, as Jane David has observed, "to articulate the goal of balancing top-down control with bottom-up authority and discretion than to determine what this means in practice" (1993, p. 3). Part of the problem stems from the fact that schools—and the government agencies that support them—have yet to become "problem-solving" organizations, as Phillip Schlechty calls them. He maintains that schools are set up to be maintainers, not innovators. Indeed, one school superintendent confessed to him that "the main opposition to KERA is from the educational community" (2001, p. 74).

Recalcitrant teachers routinely told students that it was "time to put away your books so we can do this KERA stuff," or words to that effect. One of our staff members said that in her previous private sector workplace, these teachers would have been called *transparent managers* who see their job as conveying bad news to subordinates with no personal responsibility for the message. When such managers say, "I'm telling you to do this because the front office is making me do it," employees, or students and parents, get the message: "What I'm telling you is not worthwhile. We'll just go through the motions."

MOBILIZING FOR ACTION

As an organized group of citizens, the Prichard Committee had to keep its own members committed and at the same time reach a much larger group of citizens. Our information and agenda-setting strategies helped us mobilize others, but the reverse is also true: If you don't have mobilized supporters, it's hard to set the agenda.

Public advocacy groups must enlist support for their cause over the long haul. If they are engaged in school reform, they have to overcome educators' mentality that reforms will disappear in time. Substantive school reforms might take 20 years or more to achieve ideal results, all children learning at high levels. Organizations like the Prichard Committee can help keep things on track over the long run, but that takes mobilized people.

Those in power need to know that someone is watching. High expectations help. Someone also must bridge political cycles when administrations change hands and interest wanes. One reason that complex reforms fail is that there is no reason for a new officeholder to carry them out—unless an outside group sets the expectation that they will.

So endurance is an important aspect of civic capacity. Some military historians saw George Washington as a general without brilliance. His greatest achievement, one wrote, "was keeping his army in the field" (Noland, 2000, p. D3). Here are a few rules of thumb for keeping an army in the field.

Be a Voice of Moderation Amidst Extremes

The polarized public debate over school reform that characterized the 1990s discouraged many ordinary people from getting involved. So did the technical complexity of reform and its specific elements, such as testing procedures or funding formulas. These two conditions—polarizing antireform rhetoric and confusion or doubt about reform techniques—came together to make mobilizing people particularly difficult. Our job, as we saw it, was to shape a middle ground that made sense to other citizens and encourage them to be part of the public dialogue.

The context of this debate was that the reform legislation itself was not perfect and implementation was not always smooth, effective, or wise. A number of questions arose from the start:

- Would the funding formula be fair to all school districts, including the wealthier ones?
- Could the state bureaucracy stop giving orders and let local decision making work?
- Would school councils live up to their high billing, or would they just move politics down to the school level?
- Would teachers have enough time to learn and plan?
- Would there be adequate professional development for teachers and information for schools?
- Would teaching practice really improve?
- Were the standards clear enough?

- Could the assessments, with lots of student writing, be scored accurately?
- Was the timeline for accountability too fast?
- Would school rewards be distributed effectively?
- Were the reforms too much, all at once, for the system to absorb?

As advocates, we saw ourselves as what some call "friendly critics." Our goals were to: counsel patience, point out progress, and call attention to flaws. This was not easy because the reform was "systemic"—the pieces all fit together, and all were needed. But such balance in our messages was made even more elusive by the political climate. In short, we advocated implementation but recognized that problems existed in the reform act. For us, reform was complicated; for its real critics, it wasn't complicated at all: Reform was bad for kids, antifamily, or evil.

We had been positioned since the mid-1980s as a voice from the political center. Educational improvement, not a social or cultural policy, was our only issue. Our membership was nonpartisan, a combination of private citizen activists, former governors, public intellectuals, and business leaders. The committee's party registration probably mirrored the state's (2-to-1 Democratic); 10 percent of our members were African-American; and gender division was about equal.

After the reform was passed, we saw a new twist in the education debate: the absolutist rhetoric of culture war politics. A national political movement spread terrifying warnings about school reform through radio talk shows, television ministries, the Internet and Web sites, and polarizing news reporting. The rhetoric of the culture wars that swept the nation bled into debates over standards-based reform, brought to national attention in the Pennsylvania "anti–outcomes-based education" campaign. It didn't take long for apocalyptic language to migrate to Kentucky. Expressions like *mind control, educrats, extreme environmentalism, government schools,* and *experimenting on children* entered the vocabulary for the first time.

This adversarial climate moved in like a fog over the implementation, making measured discussion, research-based change, and mobilizing of the larger public more difficult. By no means were people who considered themselves cultural conservatives the only critics of reform. ("You don't have to be a member of the Radical Flat Earth in Society to have problems with this," one of our members quipped.)

Opponents in groups with ideological agendas were, however, the only organized opposition, the ones with staff and volunteers who lobbied the legislature and whose comments the media sought.

What about other opposition? Established education associations were generally supportive, and even though they had legitimate concerns about certain reform elements, they were measured in their public criticism. Many university faculty members had objections but most of them, too, were muted. But there was worry and suspicion about reforms in the general public—among parents and voters and business people. "If you want to make enemies change something" said the message board on the street in front of a local church.

Some people disagreed with some or all of the reforms' premises. Others believed the horror stories or had partial or inaccurate information. Some disliked testing or thought writing portfolios were "makework" that couldn't be fairly graded. Others believed their children were already working too hard in school. Some people hated the ideas of financial rewards to teachers in schools that did well. Others thought the multiage primary school would hold their children back, push them too fast, be chaotic, or slight the basics. The establishment of school councils worried others who thought the principal should make all the decisions. The list could go on and on.

It was this public reaction that concerned us most and that we tried to influence. It was the general public who needed to be given comprehensible and accurate information and to hear why reform was needed.

All the stress of trying to decipher new educational language, practices, and policies converged with the upsurge of cultural conservatism. Teachers doing their best to comply with all the reforms, but who didn't always know how to explain them, were easy targets for impassioned critics and scare tactics.

It was easy to sow doubts about Kentucky's school changes. The news media often helped. For a 1992 Louisville television news special called "Radical Reform," the station's promotional spot featured a young child morphing into a guinea pig at her school desk as an announcer intoned, "This is your child on KERA." This was a powerful reinforcement of the view that school reform was a dangerous experiment of the "educrats" on defenseless children.

We compiled this television segment and other public speeches into a short video documentary because we decided that people needed to know what was being said. In one segment, a high school teacher told her audience that the Kentucky reform law had become "our state religion" and was "brainwashing" students to believe that they, not God, controlled their own destinies. In another video clip, an insurance agent earned wild applause when he said, "I see KERA as being a socialist approach to changing society." And a former parochial school teacher claimed the Prichard Committee was part of a national conspiracy to "take over the minds of American children." (I was touched several years later when the woman who said this sought me out and apologized.)

These charges drew upon growing fears of government and "government schools" and the pro-family campaigns of national political organizations. They built upon the public's already shaky confidence in public education and in reform, and fed on the impression that classrooms were dangerous and chaotic, focused only on self-esteem, not "real" learning. Absorbing emotional messages like these took no effort at all; understanding school change, on the other hand, required concentration and patience. We were forced to spend a great deal of time setting the record straight. To do this we needed to reach teachers.

Generally, teachers weren't highly visible in the ideological opposition groups. But they had their own reservations about, or outright objections to, what was going on. Regardless of their opinions, teachers were reluctant to publicly correct misinformation, sometimes because they didn't know enough themselves. Since parents and citizens trust teachers and get most of their information from them, their silence or opposition stood in the way of mobilizing citizen reform advocates.

There was no practical way to reach all teachers. Most communication with them came from the educational establishment, so it was important that local superintendents, the state department of education, and the Kentucky Education Association sent clear messages and answered teachers' questions. These sources were inclined to be helpful—the Kentucky Education Association generally supported the reform—and our role was to encourage them. Likewise, broadly targeted advertisements and publications helped by showing that reform had public support and by acknowledging teachers' frustrations. It helped, for instance, to highlight school success stories and recognize effective teachers and principals. Most of all, through our very presence and high visibility, the Committee symbolized to teachers that they had support, sympathy, and allies in the larger public. As time passed, opinion polls began to show increasing support from teachers and affirmation that a majority thought schools were getting better.

Buy Time for Change

Mobilizing more citizens as advocates for reform was essential for keeping policies from veering off and for sending a clear message that the reform will not go away. "What you're doing is buying time for the system to ingest the reforms," a foundation executive told me in

1996. His metaphor reminded me of the subtle message in a comment by former Kentucky Governor Bert Combs. When Combs was about 80 years old, people often praised him for being a "statesman." Combs responded, "It helps if you outlive your enemies." We tried to live by his metaphor.

The problem was compounded by the shifting definition of the status quo. As soon as the Kentucky Education Reform Act was passed, it became the establishment position. Reform, not schools in general, became the object of criticism for people frustrated with their schools.

We saw our job as building patience and providing protection for educators and policy makers who were trying to implement the changes by reminding people how far Kentucky's educational level had fallen before the reform law and how much higher it still must reach. As Robert Evans suggests in *The Human Side of School Change*, "One cannot hope to implement change without persuading people that it is necessary" (1996, p. 55). We also had to show that schools were making progress.

Behind the scenes we worked to counter unfounded charges and misinformation. The Kentucky Department of Education was often slow to respond to critics because officials were preoccupied with figuring out how to implement all the mandated changes. They also had to worry that legislators might retaliate on behalf of their constituents. But without an organized effort to challenge inaccuracies, the public would accept the myths as fact.

Countering misinformation is steady work. One example involves the misuse of data. For several years, a university professor had written opinion articles and granted interviews to reporters about his concerns about the high cost of the testing system mandated by the reform. In several accounts, he quoted a California scholar who, he claimed, had proved that Kentucky's testing and accountability system cost "one billion dollars." Others repeated his charge.

Although it was ludicrous on the surface to imagine that anyone believed a testing program budgeted at $8 million actually cost $1 billion, the story took life. Finally, after he used the incorrect figure in a legislative hearing, I sent an e-mail message to the California researcher, whom I had never met, asking whether he was being quoted accurately. He said that the figure in no way reflected his research. He had heard about the misuse of his data and was appalled, he said, but had not done anything about it. No one had asked him. My job, as I saw it, was to give him a vehicle.

A short time later, on a television talk show, a leading critic of the state reforms was debating the Kentucky education commissioner and cited the billion-dollar figure. Armed with a copy of the researcher's written disclaimer, the commissioner easily countered this charge. A few weeks later, however, legislative staffers informed me that the university critic had changed his story. Now he said the research proved the testing program had cost $250 million. Again, I e-mailed the researcher in California. "Do you say KIRIS costs $250 million? Is this true?" I asked. He wrote back, saying he was tired of his research being distorted and was willing to come to Kentucky to correct the false statements. We used that response too.

Later, when I talked to the education commissioner about these events, he expressed frustration that no one on his staff had ever thought to follow up on the misstatements. "They wouldn't have been that aggressive," he said. "They wouldn't have shaped the debate."

This incident suggests an important lesson that is worth repeating. It is difficult for government agencies to respond credibly and quickly in a crisis. Outside groups such as the Prichard Committee are usually better positioned to deliver quick responses.

ENGAGING PARENTS

Mobilizing and expanding our citizen base depended, in the early years of reform, on our community committees, information networks, media support, public appearances—all the strategies discussed so far. But after about 6 years, in 1996, we decided to try a new, more aggressive and focused approach.

In retrospect, I see that we had learned from experience just how much we needed different mobilizing tactics *after* reform was passed than *before*. Before reform there was a clear "enemy"—poor schools, poor education. The knowledge that volunteer reform advocates needed to make this case was quite general, personal, and emotional. After reform was enacted, with specific measures afoot in real schools, reform-minded volunteers needed more specific and detailed knowledge. Their job now was to explain, not just criticize. Our new tactic to deal with this was to mobilize parents as a specific audience via a concentrated program, the Commonwealth Institute for Parent Leadership.

We decided that standards-based reform had its own specific qualities that shaped how the public could be most effectively engaged.

Assuming people believed reform was necessary, and that they accepted the motivational power of high standards and accountability, the unique challenge came with their specific role in reforms. What was that role?

We reasoned that the reform goal in Kentucky is high levels of achievement for all students. Teachers are most responsible, but they alone cannot increase achievement for all students; parents and community members have to contribute more than they had in the past. This led us to the conclusion that we needed to see accountability as bigger than a school activity. To be an effective lever to improve learning for all students, accountability had to be a community responsibility.

But there were obstacles to such a broad definition of accountability. Communication between the public and schools, and between parents and teachers, had atrophied and often soured over the past generation. As a result, face-to-face communication had to be reestablished and school-community bonds rebuilt to renew trust between parent and teacher. In turn, we believed, this communication and trust could lead to increasing student achievement since it would help parents play their part in holding schools accountable.

Our thinking was similar to what others have observed about implementing standards-based reforms. In their study of reform in New York, for instance, Mediratta and Fruchter verify the importance of what they call "bottom-up accountability" that creates "new relationships with parents and community that foster linkages, transparency and leverage necessary to make school reform work" (2003, p. 12).

So the rationale for our new mobilizing approach went something like this:

• High achievement for all children would not be reached by schools and teachers acting alone. Both outside pressure and assistance for educators is needed, particularly from families.

• Parents, families, and communities must contribute in many ways. Achievement increases when more families and parents are engaged in their children's schools; too many are not engaged.

• The most credible communication with the public about school reform issues is one-on-one communication. The most common one-on-one form of communication is between teachers and parents. Most of the public's knowledge about schools flows outward from this personal communication between teachers and parents. Rumor and hearsay are the norm, not the exception.

• The main source of information about education and reform for the general public is what teachers tell parents. Teachers can build or undermine confidence in reform by what they say to parents.

• Useful communication between parent and teacher is limited; it is inhibited by numerous well-known barriers such as school schedules or educational jargon.

• Communication was made even more complex in Kentucky because of standards-based reform. High-stakes assessment makes standards important, not cosmetic; but the link between state-imposed student assessment and student achievement was not clear to parents and teachers. The standards themselves were new and often vague and hard for teachers as well as parents to understand. In addition, the emotional political debate increased parent and teacher confusion about standards.

• Parents process what they hear from teachers based on whatever knowledge they have to start with. Parent knowledge, however, is often quite limited; they know little about their child's academic achievement other than what they see in school report cards and hear in conferences with teachers.

• Parents must be armed with knowledge and skills so they can communicate effectively with teachers and school personnel about student achievement and act effectively on behalf of their own children.

• Parents also need to realize that all children in their school must learn, not just their own child, if their school is to be considered successful.

• As a result, the Prichard Committee's organizing/communication strategies must become more focused on this one-on-one conversation between parents and educators, supplemented by individual volunteer activities. These activities must be based on objectives that a parent volunteer can complete and feel good about and that improve achievement for all students in the school.

• Enhancing this one-on-one communication by energized and informed parents will lead to a larger army of self-confident and informed volunteer activists who will gather others and insist that reforms are implemented. This army will be composed of parents who have the tools they need to help improve their schools.

Following from this rationale we decided that our objective of reaching the public would be more achievable if our audience was more tightly targeted. Our approach was to create the most ambitious project we had undertaken, the Commonwealth Institute for Parent

Leadership. The institute would (1) focus on parents as a subset of the larger public, (2) pull together parent mobilizing activities under one internal umbrella, and (3) shine a public spotlight on parents as an outside force to push schools and teachers toward increasing student achievement.

For the Prichard Committee, the graduates of the institute were to be a revitalized cadre of local volunteers. These graduates are linked together through various gatherings, publications, and communication. Their activities are managed by regional coordinators, who operate out of home offices. As a side benefit, these energetic and enthusiastic staff members also expand our statewide presence by visiting schools, meeting with civic groups and leaders, and generally proselytizing for the reforms' implementation.

Funding from national and state donors enabled us to train and support about 200 parents each year starting in 1997. Six days of training was designed and conducted by the committee's staff. It focused on understanding reform (particularly school achievement data), organizing other parents, helping teachers improve achievement, and creating a sustainable initiative in their schools.

Every parent designed a personal project during training; we helped to carry it out with coaching from our regional staff. Parent projects ranged from establishing reading programs to transition programs for middle school students, to setting up electronic homework hotlines, to attacking the achievement gap in schools with high poverty rates.

It was by watching the institute that I fully understood the power of school achievement data. Our training concentrates heavily on helping parents understand their own school's data and seeing how it might lead to changed emphasis or instruction in their school. Parents first immerse in the theory and mechanics of the larger reform and assessment, setting the context for the end product—understanding their school data. Then we give them specially prepared, user-friendly, reports on their own schools. These customized reports show change over time, differences in subject areas, and results by race, economic condition, and gender. They can readily compare their school's results with those of other parents at the table; they can easily see whether "all" children are progressing in their school and compare it to other schools. The effect is palpable and instant. The lightbulbs over heads are almost visible. And, since they now have information (and understand it) that many educators in their schools don't have or haven't used, they gain confidence.

In addition to leading these initiatives, Commonwealth Institute graduates use their training to take on official roles shaping school policy. Nearly 400 graduates have been elected to positions on school councils or local school boards. Others serve on consolidated planning and other school policy-making committees. Dozens more serve on various state boards or task forces. An annual directory of all graduates since 1997 is sent to journalists who might be looking for parent comments in stories and to state officials who might be looking for parents to appoint to boards and commissions.

Two things distinguish these parents from other "engaged parents": their connection to an advocacy organization, the Prichard Committee, and their concentration on increasing student achievement. They need help and encouragement, of course, so our staff's job is to provide it, linking them to like-minded volunteers or experts, gathering them together periodically, visiting their schools—whatever it takes.

An outside evaluation of the institute found that the focus on achievement "steered parents away from their traditional role of being passive responders to school requests and pushed them toward being active advocates for improved academics for all students . . . (that) quite noticeably sets them apart from other parents" (Corbett & Wilson, 2000, p. 41).

Through the institute, we are also merging the concepts of engaging the public with that of engaging parents, often seen by scholars as competing activities. Heather Voke, for instance, who writes for the Association for Supervision and Curriculum Development, has argued that "public engagement is different from parental engagement in that it is motivated by a commitment to secure a quality education for *all* children rather than for one's *own* children only" (2002, p. 1). Our push via the institute showed us this does not have to be true if parents are given the right information, tools, and support.

The Commonwealth Institute for Parent Leadership was, by far, our most substantial effort to reach parents, but there were others. Already mentioned were our Parents and Teachers Talking Together conversations, where trained volunteer facilitators conducted structured dialogues in hundreds of schools. In Jefferson County, the state's largest district, a group of parents, with support from the Edna McConnell Clark Foundation, also pushed for middle school improvement through what we called a County Accountability Team (CAT). The group reviewed state achievement data, disaggregated the data to show disparities, and brought it to the public's attention. They followed up on their research with an in-depth study of five schools and issued a report to the community. Although the CAT group was sometimes frustrated with the pace of improvement in the district, there is little doubt that heightened the district's focus on learning gaps in middle schools and increased dialogue between school administrators and parents. One result of this increased attention was that a state senator championed and got legislation passed that requires the state to disaggregate test data by race and income and required school councils to address any gaps that were found. (Lewis, 2002; Liebman & Sabel, 2003).

CONCLUSION

Compared to many other states, people in Kentucky have been able to debate complex reform topics without discarding core reform measures. The initial vision of all children learning at high levels and of reforms based on standards, assessment, accountability, local decision making, and increased resources has by and large been maintained.

All of the strategies discussed in this chapter converge at a single point: staying focused. This focus has, in a rough and general way, been maintained. There has been disagreement. There have been changes; some changes have strengthened and some have weakened the initial program. But mostly, the implementation of reform has stayed on the trail that was marked in 1990.

This continued focus occurred because of several factors:

- A united educational community
- A core of committed legislators
- Continuity of viewpoint in the governor's office
- A generally supportive and attentive media
- Support from mainstream civic organizations
- Consistent public support

All of these depended on the public and voters. Starting in the early 1990s, opinion polls showed that a plurality of the public supported reform and that most people thought that reform would result in better schools. A sense of positive possibilities and pride began to emerge; a college student told me that Kentucky was developing an "attitude of success, not survival."

In governor's races, no candidate in the 1991, 1995, or 1999 elections made opposition to the Kentucky Education Reform Act a key issue in their campaigns. (Both parties' candidates in two of these elections had, at one time, been members of the Prichard Committee.)

Focus was maintained by other strategies as well. Alliances that had been established in the 1980s were continued through the 1990s. The media were provided with extensive information. Consistent themes were maintained; distractions were minimized. Bridges were built between political administrations and leadership transitions in the Kentucky Department of Education.

Citizens were at the table when changes were made, such as those in assessment and accountability. Radical and destructive proposals were countered with less harmful alternatives. New items were added to the reform agenda, such as teacher preparation and professional development, stronger reading instruction, and early childhood reforms.

Focus was also influenced by research, although the Prichard Committee was not a research organization. Instead, it helped create the Kentucky Institute for Education Research. Keeping that institute strong over time became an important part of our own agenda.

In short, politicians, educators, and the media stayed focused on the ends and the means that were established in 1990. The dominant discussion was about finding solutions within the existing reform framework, not starting over. There were steps forward and steps backward, but compared to many other states, direction and momentum was maintained.

CHAPTER 8

Summing Up:
The Lessons Learned

Every critic is an apologist-in-waiting.

—Alan Wolfe

Many people believe that Kentucky's passage of the Education Reform Act was solely the result of the Supreme Court's 1989 decision, but this interpretation is too simple. A more complex collection of forces was at work through the 1980s, long before the court ruled. These forces set the stage for the court's ruling and the comprehensive reform that resulted.

Six years of media and public outrage about the inadequacies of Kentucky's educational system had created favorable conditions for this historic effort and had generated the necessary support for a high-stakes political action, a difficult and complex reform, and a large tax increase. Through it all, the Prichard Committee was a focal point. Its advocacy both fed on and reflected the public's frustration with inadequate public schools.

But the situation changed after reforms were enacted in 1990. Clearly, it is pointless to advocate for something you won't defend. But, just as clearly, the outraged spoke louder, had a simpler message, and had more to say than the satisfied. Before 1990, poor schools were the source of outrage for the Prichard Committee and its friends, and their energy was fueled by that outrage. After 1990, the new reforms became the enemy for a different group of people, and their passion was ignited.

Advocates and organizers know that maintaining energy is hard work in the face of either defeat or victory. Those who advocated for reform had won; could their enthusiasm be maintained, or would it become "like a match under wet wood"? But energy was sustained, and somehow enough Kentucky citizens concluded that passing a reform law wasn't enough. They decided that classroom improvement would be harder than passing legislation, and they stayed focused for 12 more years.

Our experience shows that the public doesn't rise up to slay dragons easily. Someone has to carry the flag—to organize, to synthesize, to strategize, to bring coherence, to keep the focus. That's what the citizens on the Prichard Committee and their like-minded friends have attempted to do.

There is growing evidence that comprehensive state-level reforms based on standards are starting to make a difference, albeit a slowly evolving one. Where there has been educational progress, writes Susan Fuhrman, it's because there has been enough political stability to weather inevitable false starts, retreats, and restarts. "The bottom line is that these findings offer hope for continued educational improvement if enough political stability can be created to sustain the standards agenda and if policymakers come to realize that accountability is not enough" (2001, p. 277).

It is important for both political stability and an expanded view of reform that people outside of the system pay attention. This is the civic capacity discussed in this book. The Prichard Committee acted as a surrogate for other citizens when they did the following:

- Created a sense of urgency and reminded the public continuously why the reforms were needed
- Represented the public in state policy discussions, assuming an aggressive monitoring role and countering the tendency to veer off from the reform's original intent
- Helped parents become stronger advocates for their children and other children in their schools
- Reinforced the commitment of the business community to Kentucky's school reforms
- Kept the public focused on results and kept the reform on track
- Kept a network of 7,000 citizens engaged and supportive

What were the results? Student achievement on the state's assessment and on the National Assessment of Educational Progress (NAEP) has risen steadily. Kentucky is one of just a few states (with North Carolina, Texas, Connecticut, and Maryland) to have significant gains on NAEP in several subjects. An achievement gap persists, however, and economically disadvantaged schools have not improved enough.

The lessons we've learned about building civic capacity and mobilizing the public and parents as school reform advocates would be useful guidelines for other advocacy groups.

- *Get people's attention.* If people give you their attention, they're giving you a great compliment and considerable power. There is much symbolic value in getting people's attention. Our board chair got it right when he mused, "It sometimes is a miracle to me that people have embraced us and used us as their spokesperson without being involved in creating us."
- *Set a clear, but not necessarily detailed, agenda.* We started out by collecting our own thoughts about how to improve schools as citizens and made our own statement about Kentucky's educational problems and our own recommendations for solving those problems. That took the form of a published report; it was a 2-year process. Setting our own agenda and laying out a compelling vision meant that we were redefining a negative situation as one that people could do something about.
- *Be a symbol of hope.* People will not do any of this unless they think there is a chance for success. Let people know about good results—fuel a sense of historic moment.
- *Engage people on a personal level.* Someone told me the Prichard Committee translated ideas to the public, but that was not wholly accurate. We were asking the public to do the work themselves. The "we" was literally hundreds of volunteers. We educated ourselves. Our citizen volunteers studied the issues, read tedious research, listened to experts, and met about 65 times in the early 2-year period as we wrote our first report. In the process we engaged others and created a statewide public classroom on education reform. Anyone could enroll.
- *Build and maintain credibility by protecting your independence.* People must believe that you are sincere; they must give you their trust; and they must take you seriously. Deeds—not image—are the source of deep credibility. Deeds must show that there is no hidden political agenda. Deeds must show that you are above partisan and electoral politics even as you show that you have political skills.
- *Give credit to others.* Giving credit builds credibility partly because it is the opposite of the behavior of candidates for office and partly because it builds trust. Given the current atmosphere of distrust for government, giving credit to officials or politicians who do good work is essential.
- *Maintain cooperative, open relationships with the media.*

News coverage of education in all its aspects, including its problems, is required. The more coverage the better, and the more detailed, the better still.

• *Meet people's needs.* Respond to people who need you through hands-on work in communities, and provide quality help and information to those who request it.

• *Provide responsible ideas that make sense.* This means writing reports, using research, providing comments in the media, and reaching out to other constituencies who need information. Many organizations weaken their credibility by complaining and criticizing but suggesting nothing to solve the problems they bemoan. Ideas must engage people's emotions without being demagogic. Our voice, joined by others, created a sense of possibility. As the implementation stage unfolds, seeking the balance between ideas and advocacy becomes more difficult.

• *Pick issues and fights strategically.* The rule is focus, focus, focus—what media consultants call *staying on message.* Focusing means declining to fight, however tempting the invitation, over hot-button topics that some people love to fight about. Countless social issues are available for debate, but every topic bearing on schooling doesn't have equal power to improve student achievement. Focusing doesn't mean being rigid. Flexibility is also a key to success, particularly as focus becomes more difficult because of changing political conditions.

• *Create a web of relationships.* Emphasize building and maintaining creative alliances with other advocates, educators, civic groups, business people—anyone who can lend a hand. Alliances take care and feeding, but they're vital. Keep everybody connected to everybody else.

• *Be persistent.* "The leader's job is to hold the vision," said one of our activist members. Remember Woody Allen's quip, "Ninety-five percent of success is just showing up." It's critical that reform advocates publicly commit to being there until the job is done. Those in authority—and those in opposition—most certainly will be there. Persistence is tough. Volunteers get tired. Money is hard to find. And when reform is in place, the toughest work has started.

• *Stay focused yourself so everybody else can stay focused.*

By the yardstick of comparison with other states, I believe that Kentucky citizens who cared about good schools have done well. As a large group of volunteers, they knew they were at the center of what a major newspaper called "the most important sustained effort in modern Kentucky history to change the state's culture and the economic prospects of young people" ("Partnership Returns," 2001, p. A8). The experiences of these volunteer citizens are a hopeful sign about building public support for improved public schools. Their experience shows that people will get involved if the stakes are compelling and they believe the chances for improvement are realistic.

These volunteers have shown that commitment, focus, and inclusiveness can produce outstanding results. They shared a deep faith in the power of high-quality education. They trusted in the possibility of progress, even against discouraging conditions. They could envision a better way and knew that they and their fellow citizens could reach it. They believed that they owned a big share of government and felt personally responsible for making sure it served them and other people well. They were doers, not complainers, who kept their eyes on the prize. Like General Washington, they kept their army in the field.

Afterword

This story never ends. Even as this book is published, the reforms face their most serious challenge yet.

Kentucky's revenue shortfalls and budget cuts, common to all states, gave reform opponents the opportunity to eliminate certain reform elements, particularly those related to accountability, in the 2003 legislative session. These included reallocating the trust fund containing financial rewards for school improvement (with the promise that they will be restored in the future); eliminating regional service centers that provide professional development and help struggling schools; and stripping funds from the department of education that allowed it to provide management assistance to school districts in bankrupt conditions.

These backward steps, while not fatal individually, remove pieces of the larger systemic infrastructure that undergirds the comprehensive reforms in Kentucky. It is likely, many people feel, that this push against reform will grow stronger, fueled by continued revenue shortfalls, inadequate education funding, and the implementation of the No Child Left Behind Act of 2001. The result may be the most serious push since its enactment to roll back the Kentucky Education Reform Act.

Budget shortfalls and the structural inadequacies of the state's revenue system are the most powerful weapons the antireform elements have had yet because they provide political cover for eliminating reforms piecemeal. Meanwhile, as several studies have shown, state funding is also no longer adequate for schools to reach the goal of all children learning at high levels established in 1990. Inadequate funding, in turn, weakens the bargain between educators and taxpayers: "We'll accept your demand for improvement," educators said, "in return for the resources required to do it."

In response, the education community and concerned citizens and business leaders have joined together in an unprecedented alliance representing early childhood, elementary and secondary, postsecondary and adult education plus civic and business organizations. Their goals are these:

- Present a common education agenda
- Persuade the legislature to provide adequate revenue linked to accountability
- Conduct a coordinated public campaign leading up to the 2004 legislative session

The Prichard Committee was asked to convene this group and to facilitate its activities.

For its own part, the Prichard Committee, with the encouragement and support of several national foundations, is seeking to build its own financial capacity to sustain its advocacy work. To do that it has created Parent Leadership Associates, a consulting division in partnership with KSA-Plus Communications, to work with clients outside Kentucky who want to engage parents and citizens as advocates.

References

ACCESS (Advocacy Center for Children's Educational Success with Standards). (2001). *Civic engagement and educational standards: Implications of Campaign for Fiscal Equity vs. State of New York.* Selected Readings. New York: Author.

Adams, J. E., Jr. (1993). *The Prichard Committee for Academic Excellence: Credible advocacy for Kentucky schools.* Philadelphia: Consortium for Policy Research in Education.

Adams, J. E., Jr. (2003). Results of retrenchment: The real race in American educational reform. *New York University Review of Law and Social Change.*

Annenberg Institute. (n.d.) *Reason for hope, voices for change.* Providence, RI: Author.

Ashland Oil to promote town forums on education. (1984, October 19). *Lexington Herald Leader,* p. C11.

Bradley, A. (1998, March 25). Public engagement said to hold promise for schools. *Education Week, 17*(28), 10.

Bush lauds Kentucky for efforts to reform schools. (1990, April 5). *Lexington Herald-Leader,* p. A8.

The Business Roundtable. (1998). *Building support for tests that count: A business leader's guide.* Washington, DC: Author.

Building from the blueprint. (1982, June 8). *Lexington Herald,* A12.

Bush lauds Kentucky for efforts to reform schools. (1990, April 15).

Campbell, T. (1998). *Short of the glory.* Lexington: University Press of Kentucky.

Corbett, D., & Wilson, B. (2000, December 12). I didn't know I could do that: Parents learning to be leaders through the Commonwealth Institute for Parent Leadership. Philadelphia: Pew Charitable Trusts.

Cross, A. (1995, October 8). The race for governor: Listening to Kentucky: Voters skeptical, yearn for details as election nears. *Louisville Courier-Journal,* p. 1A.

Darling-Hammond, L. (1998, January-February). Teachers and teaching: Testing policy hypothesis from a national commission report. *Educational Researcher, 27,*(1), 5–15.

Davenport, G. (1998, January 7). Letter to the Editor. *Louisville Courier-Journal,* p. A12.

David, J. (1993). *Redesigning an education system: Early observations from*

Kentucky. Washington, DC: National Governors Association and the Prichard Committee for Academic Excellence.

David, J. (1997). Pew Network for standards based reform: Year one evaluation report. Menlo Park, CA: SRI International.

Duggan, T., & Holmes, M. (2000). *Closing the gap,* Washington, DC: Council for Basic Education.

Elmore, R. (1996) Getting to scale with successful educational practices. In S. Fuhrman & Jennifer A. O'Day (Eds.), *Rewards and reform: Creating educational incentives that work* (pp. 294–329). San Francisco: Jossey-Bass.

Elmore, R., & McLaughlin, M. W. (1998) *Steady work: Policy, practice and the reform of American education.* Santa Monica, CA: Rand Corporation.

Evans, R. (1996) *The human side of school change: Reform, resistance, and the real-life problems of innovations.* San Francisco: Jossey-Bass.

Farkas, S., Foley, P., & Duffett, A. (with Foleno, T., & Johnson, J.). (2001). *Just waiting to be asked: A fresh look at attitudes on public engagement.* New York: Public Agenda Foundation.

First event in push for better schools draws 400. (1984, October 10). *Louisville Courier-Journal,* p. A1.

Fiske, E. B. (1990, March 30) Kentucky acts to reorganize school system. *New York Times,* p. A1.

Fiske, E. B. (1990, April 4). Lessons. *New York Times,* p. B6.

Fruchter, N., & Jarvis, C. (1995, September 5). *An assessment of the Prichard Committee's community committees for education.* New York: New York University, Institute for Education and Social Policy.

Fuhrman, S. (1994). *Politics and systemic education reform* (Policy Brief). Philadelphia, PA: Consortium for Policy Research in Education.

Fuhrman, S. (Ed.). (2001). *From Capitol to the classroom: Standards based reform in the States.* 100th Yearbook of the National Society for the Study of Education. Chicago: University of Chicago Press.

Fullan, M. (1993). *Change forces: Probing the depths of educational change.* London: Falmer Press.

Fullan, M., Galluzzo, G., Morris, P., & Watson, N. (2001). *The rise and stall of education reform.* Washington, DC: American Association of Colleges of Teacher Education.

Gittell, M. J. (Ed.). (1998). *Strategies for school equity.* New Haven, CT: Yale University Press.

Governor and legislators open the way for march towards better education. (1984, November 6). *Louisville Courier-Journal,* p. A12.

Harp, L. (1997). No place to go but up. *Education Week's Quality Counts.* Washington, DC: Editorial Projects in Education.

Harwood, R. C. (1996, January). *The public realm: Where America must address its concerns.* The Harwood Group Series, Vol. 1, no. 1. Bethesda, MD: The Harwood Institute.

Healy, F. H., & DeStefano, J. (1997). *Education reform support: A framework for scaling up school reform.* Research Triangle Park, NC: Research Triangle Institute.

Heifetz, R. A. (1994). *Leadership without easy answers*. Cambridge, MA: Belknap Press.

Heine, C. (1992). *The school answer book: A citizens' guide to Kentucky school law* (2nd Ed.). Lexington, KY: Prichard Committee for Academic Excellence.

Henderson, A., & Berla, N. (1994). *A new generation of evidence: The family is critical to school achievement*. Washington, DC: Center for Law and Education.

Hill, P. (2001, Spring). Good schools for big city children. *Helping Committees Work Smarter for Kids* no. 7. Seattle: Urban Health Initiative.

Hirshberg, C. (1999, Sept.). How good are our schools? *Life, 22*(10), p. 40.

Holland, H. (1998). *Making change: Three educators join the battle for better schools*. Portsmouth, NH: Heinemann.

Hornbeck, D. (2000, December 7). Presentation to conference of Kentucky Institute for Education Research (KIER). Louisville, KY.

Hunter, M. (1999). All eyes forward: Public engagement and educational reform in Kentucky. *Journal of Law and Education, 28*(4), 485–516.

A job that isn't finished. (1982, June 8). *Louisville Courier-Journal*, p. A14.

Kannapel, P., Moore, B., Coe, P., Aagaard, L. (1995, April 19). *Opposition to Outcome-Based Education in Kentucky*. Charleston, WV: Appalachian Educational Laboratory.

Kentucky's bold school reform. (1990, April 14). *San Antonio Express News*, p. B4.

Kentucky's class act. (1997, April 7). *Business Week*, pp. 90–91.

Lewis, A. C., (2002, August). *Community accountability team in Louisville: Waking a sleeping giant*. New York: Edna McConnell Clark Foundation.

Liebman, J. S., & Sabel, C. F. (2003). A public laboratory Dewey barely imagined: The emerging model of school governance and legal reform, *New York University Review of Law and Social Change, 28*(2).

Manno, B. (2000, December 7). Presentation to conference of the Kentucky Institute for Education Research (KIER). Louisville, KY.

Margolis, Jon. (1996, July 22). Washington watch. *High Country News*, p. 7.

Mathews, D. (1990). *Politics is for people* (2nd ed.). Chicago: University of Illinois Press.

Mathews, D. (1996). *Is there a public for public schools?* Dayton, OH: Kettering Foundation Press.

Mathews, D. (1999, June). Whose schools? Reconnecting the public and public schools. *American School Board Journal, 186*, 22–24.

Mayer, J. (2002, June 27). True confessions. *New York Review of Books*, p. 6.

Mediratta, K., & Fruchter, N. (2003). *From governance to accountability: Building relationships that make schools work*. New York: Drum Major Institute for Public Policy.

Morgan, V. (1997, Sept. 24). School attendance incentives: Bribes or rewards. *Louisville Courier-Journal*, p. A1.

Morone, James A. (2003). *Hellfire nation: The politics of sin in American history*. New Haven, CT: Yale University Press.

National Governors Association. (1994). *Communicating with the public about education reform.* Washington, DC: Author.

National Research Council. (1999). *Testing, teaching, and learning: A guide for states and school districts.* (Committee on Title I Testing and Assessment, Richard F. Elmore and Robert Rothman, editors. Board on Testing and Assessment, Commission on Behavioral and Social Sciences and Education.) Washington, DC: National Academy Press.

Nelson, K. C. (1996). Presentation to Georgia Partnership for Excellence in Education, Atlanta, GA.

Neufeld, B. (1997, February). *Update memo: Standards-based middle school reform in the Jefferson County Public Schools.* Cambridge, MA: Education Matters.

Neufeld, B. (1998). *Standards-Based Reform in the Jefferson County Public Schools.* Cambridge, MA: Education Matters.

Neustadt, R. (1997). The politics of mistrust. In J. S. Nye, P. D. Zelikow, & D. C. King (Eds.), *Why people don't trust government* (pp. 179–202). Cambridge, MA: Harvard University Press.

Noland, T. E., Jr. (2000, January 2). Washington, Lincoln and Lee. *Louisville Courier-Journal,* p. D3.

Nye, J. S., Zelikow, P. D., King, D. C. (Eds.). (1997). *Why people don't trust government.* Cambridge, MA: Harvard University Press.

Orren, G. (1997). Fall from grace: The public's loss of faith in government. In J. S. Nye, P. D. Zelikow, & D. C. King, *Why people don't trust government* (pp. 77–108). Cambridge, MA: Harvard University Press.

Page, C. (1996, April 14). "Horse race" political coverage. *Louisville Courier-Journal,* p. D3.

Paris, M. (2001). Legal mobilization and the politics of reform: Lessons from school finance litigation in Kentucky, 1984–1995. *Law and Social Inquiry, 26*(3), 631–684.

Parrish, T. (1990). *The Prichard Committee for Academic Excellence: The first decade, 1980–1990.* Lexington, KY: Prichard Committee.

Partisanship's return. (2001, October 9). *Louisville Courier-Journal,* p. A8.

Prichard Committee for Academic Excellence. (1983). *What must be done.* Lexington, KY: Author.

Prichard Committee for Academic Excellence. (1985). *Report on town forums.* Lexington, KY: Author.

Prichard Committee for Academic Excellence. (1987). *The path to a larger life* (2nd ed.). Lexington: University Press of Kentucky.

Prichard Committee for Academic Excellence. (1990). *Where do we go from here?* Lexington, KY: Author.

Prichard Committee for Academic Excellence. (1999). Commonwealth Institute for Parent Leadership propels parents into powerful position. *Parent Leader, 1*(2), 4.

Prichard made lasting mark on education. (1984, December 24). *Lexington Herald-Leader,* p. A12.

Prichard panel says education needs tax hike. (1985, March 26). *State Journal*, (Frankford, KY), p. 5.

Puriefoy, W. D. (2000, April). All for all. *American School Board Journal, 187*, 36–38.

Riordon, W. L. (1963). *Plunkitt of Tammany Hall.* New York: Dutton.

Roberts, N., & King, P. (1996). *Transforming public policy.* San Francisco: Jossey-Bass.

Rosenberg, J. (1985, January 2). Test of commitment. *Floyd County Times*, p. 2.

Rosenstiel, T. (1997, September 14). *Washington Post*, p. CO3.

Schlechty, P. (2001). *Shaking up the school house.* San Francisco: Jossey-Bass.

Scott, J. C. (1998). *Seeing like a state.* New Haven, CT: Yale University Press.

(T. Scott, letter to Wade Mountz, March 29, 1990)

Sexton, R. F. (1999, September). *Fighting illiteracy in Kentucky schools.* Lexington, KY: Prichard Committee for Academic Excellence.

Sexton, R. F. (2000). *Whose poor scores are they?* Lexington: KY: Prichard Committee for Academic Excellence.

Sexton, R. F., & Clements, S. (1996, December). Trends and issues affecting primary and secondary education. In M. T. Childress et al. (Eds.), Exploring the Frontier of the Future (pp. 85–93). Frankfort, KY: The Kentucky Long-Term Policy Research Center, p. 89.

Shanker, A. (1990, May 6). Kentucky's school reform law. *New York Times.*

State's town forums could help shape schools of the future. (1984, November 16). *Louisville Courier-Journal*, pp. A1–13, B1, B3.

Stephens, R., Chief Justice. (1989, June 8). John A. Rose et al versus the Council for Better Education, Inc. S. W. 2d-(Ky, June 8, 1989). (No. 88-SC-804-TG).

Stone, C. (Ed.). (1998). *Changing urban education.* Lawrence: University Press of Kansas.

Taylor, C. M. (1998, Summer). *Effective strategies for the design and evaluation of media campaigns.* Philadelphia: Pew Charitable Trusts.

"Town forums" bombarded with ideas. (1984, November 16). *Louisville Times*, pp. A1–13.

Tyack, D., & Cuban, L. (1995). *Tinkering toward utopia: A century of public school reform.* Cambridge, MA: Harvard University Press.

Voke, H. (2002, July). Engaging the public in its schools. *Infobrief* (Association for Supervision and Curriculum Development), No. 30.

Walker, R. (1990, April 11). Kentucky educators hail bill's reforms—and new money. *Education Week*, p. 1, 20.

Walt, S. M. (1988, September). The hidden nature of systems. *Atlantic Monthly, 272*(3), 131–132.

Wolfe, A. (1996). *Marginal in the middle.* Chicago: University of Chicago Press.

Wolfe, A. (2000, December 11). Subject matter matters. *New Republic, 223*(24), 38–41.

For Further Reading

A full bibliography of Prichard Committee materials and publications about the Committee can be found at www.prichardcommittee.org.

Annenberg Institute for School Reform. (2002, June). *School communities that work for results and equity: A national task force on the future of urban districts*. Providence, RI: Author.

Braatz, J., & Putnam, R. D. (1998, March). *Community-based social capital and educational performance: Exploring new evidence*. Cambridge, MA: Kennedy School of Government.

Corcoran, T., & Christman, J. B. (2002). *The limits and contradictions of systemic reform: The Philadelphia story*. Philadelphia: Consortium for Policy Research in Education.

Gittell, M., Petrovich, J., & Sargent, J. (2001). *Constituency building and advocacy for education reform: A collection of seminar papers*. New York: Howard Samuels State Management and Policy Center, City University of New York.

Harvard Family Research Project. (2000, May). *The Prichard Committee for Academic Excellence: Building capacity for public engagement in education reform*. Cambridge, MA: Author.

Hirota, J. M., & Jacobs, L. E. (2003). *Vital voices: Building constituencies for public school reform*. New York: Academy for Education Development; and Chicago: Chapin Hall Center for Children.

Hochschild, J., & Scovrowick, N. (2003). *The American dream and public schools*. New York: Oxford University Press.

Mathews, D. (1997, June). The lack of a public for public schools. *Phi Delta Kappan*, 741–742.

Mediratta, K., Fruchter, N., & Lewis, A. C. (2002, October). *Organizing for school reform: How communities are finding their voices and reclaiming their public schools*. New York: Institute for Education and Social Policy, New York University.

Pankratz, R., & Petrosko, J. M. (Eds.). (2000). *All children can learn*. San Francisco: Jossey-Bass.

Research for Action. (2002). *Policy brief: Lessons from Philadelphia about building civic capacity for school reform*. Philadelphia: Author.

Rothman, R. (2002/03, Winter). "Intermediary organizations" help bring reform to scale. *Journal of the Annenberg Challenge, 6*(2).

Sexton, R. F. (2000). Engaging parents in school reform. In R. Pankratz &
J. M. Petrosko (Eds.), *All children can learn* (pp. 244–262). San Francisco:
Jossey-Bass.

Soloman, R. N., & Rhodes, A. (2002). *Strong images and practical ideas: A
guide to parent engagement in school reform.* Baltimore: Annie E. Casey
Foundation.

Index

About the Author

Robert F. Sexton has been the Executive Director of the Prichard Committee for Academic Excellence since it began in 1980. A native of Louisville, Kentucky and educated in public schools there, he graduated from Yale University and the University of Washington with a doctoral degree in history. He served as a visiting scholar at Harvard University.

Recognized across the nation for his leadership in improving public schools, he has received the Charles A. Dana Prize for Pioneering Achievement and honorary degrees from three Kentucky universities. He is an active board member and advisor to national education organizations and foundations and has worked with several initiatives to improve civic engagement, including the Saguaro Seminar on Civic Involvement.